ISAAC ABRAVANEL

ISAAC ABRAVANEL

Six Lectures

by

PAUL GOODMAN   L. RABINOWITZ
I. G. LLUBERA   L. STRAUSS
M. GASTER   A. R. MILBURN

With an Introductory Essay by
H. LOEWE

Edited by

J. B. TREND, M.A.
Professor of Spanish, Fellow of Christ's College
and

H. LOEWE, M.A.
Reader in Rabbinics, Honorary Fellow of Queens' College

CAMBRIDGE
AT THE UNIVERSITY PRESS
1937

CAMBRIDGE
UNIVERSITY PRESS

University Printing House, Cambridge CB2 8BS, United Kingdom

Cambridge University Press is part of the University of Cambridge.

It furthers the University's mission by disseminating knowledge in the pursuit of education, learning and research at the highest international levels of excellence.

www.cambridge.org
Information on this title: www.cambridge.org/9781107502086

© Cambridge University Press 1937

First published 1937
First paperback edition 2015

A catalogue record for this publication is available from the British Library

ISBN 978-1-107-50208-6 Paperback

CONTENTS

Preface   *page* vij

Isaac Abravanel and his Age   xj
BY H. LOEWE

I Introduction   I
BY PAUL GOODMAN, F.R.HIST.SOC.

II Spain in the Age of Abravanel   17
BY PROFESSOR I. GONZÁLEZ LLUBERA, *Professor
of Spanish, Queen's University, Belfast*

III Abravanel's Literary Work   39
BY DR M. GASTER, *Haham Emeritus*

IV Abravanel as Exegete   75
BY DR L. RABINOWITZ

V On Abravanel's Philosophical Tendency and   93
Political Teaching
BY DR L. STRAUSS

VI Leone Ebreo and the Renaissance   131
BY A. R. MILBURN, M.A., *Fellow of King's College*

PLATES

FACING PAGE

Eleanor of Toledo   44

Illustrated Haggadah for Passover, with Abravanel's
abbreviated commentary (*Ṣeli 'Esh*), Venice, 1629   51

Abravanel's commentary on Deuteronomy, Sabbionetta, 1551   78

Abravanel's Dissertation on kingship (Deut. xvii, 14–
20; I Sam. viii), with Latin translation by J. Buxtorf
junior, from Ugolini, *Thesaurus Antiquitatum*, Venice,
1761   111

PREFACE

The quingentenary of the birth of ISAAC ABRAVANEL has attracted much attention in academic institutions, both in Europe and in America, especially in the South American States of Iberian origin. It is impossible to enumerate the functions that have been arranged. Abravanel was a man of many parts. His life work is of interest to historians, to biblical exegetes, to students of political theory and, naturally, also to students of Rabbinics and to the Jewish communities. Hence it follows that the anniversary of his birth has been the occasion of numerous celebrations. Since the month in which he was born is not known, the functions have been held on no uniform date, and to collect a list of them would be a matter of considerable difficulty. It must suffice to enumerate only a few of them.

The impetus to the celebrations may be said to have originated with Dr Alfred Klee, who organized a highly successful Abravanel Exhibition at the Jewish Museum in Berlin. No doubt there are other claimants to the honour of priority, since, as the works of Abravanel enjoy so much popularity, the idea must have occurred to more than one student of his works. Dr Klee's Catalogue, which contains, among the etchings, a contemporary picture of Lisbon and reproductions of some of the first editions of Abravanel's works, is both historically and artistically valuable and has already become a rare pamphlet. The editors wish to express their thanks to him for the loan of the blocks reproduced in this volume.

In London, the Anglo-Jewish community held a special commemorative service in the ancient Synagogue of the Spanish and Portuguese Congregation at Bevis Marks; the sermon, delivered by the Senior Minister, the Rev. David Bueno de Mesquita, B.A., has been published. The Jewish Historical Society of England organized a series of lectures which will be printed in the *Transactions* of the Society.

At Tartu (Dorpat), a celebration, in connection with the Chair of Judaica, occupied by Prof. L. Gulkowitsch, was held in the Aula of the University, in the presence of the Rector and University officials, when a lecture was delivered by Mr P. Goodman, F.R.Hist.Soc., the Secretary of the Spanish and Portuguese Congregation, *Kahal Kados Sahar Asamaim*: we are indeed glad that Mr Goodman has been able to contribute to this volume. His knowledge of Iberian-Jewish history, his numerous writings on the subject and, above all, his practical work for the revival of Judaism among the Marranos, whom he has helped to return to their ancestral faith, entitle him to the first place in our series of lectures. It is mainly through his efforts that the quingentenary will be marked in Oporto by the opening, in December, of a Synagogue for the Marranos. This building has now been completed by the munificence of Sir Elly Kadoorie of Shanghai.

The Cambridge Hebrew Congregation had arranged a commemoration service for 14 November, when Dr Gaster, the learned *Haham Emeritus* of the Spanish and Portuguese Congregation, was to have preached. Unfortunately, ill-health prevented his visit. His lecture on Abravanel's works was delivered by his son, Mr T. H. Gaster. An Abravanel service was held on the following Saturday (21 November) and the sermon preached by Rabbi Dr Rabinowitz.

It has been our privilege to welcome Prof. Llubera of Belfast, who has made a profound study of the Hebrew elements in Spanish literature, as is evidenced by his edition of *Shemtob's Maxims* and the *Coplas de Yoçef*. He gives an outline of the Iberian background against which the life and work of Abravanel must be viewed.

Dr Rabinowitz has given a careful analysis of Abravanel's exegetical method. His Bible Commentaries attracted probably more Christian translators than did those of any other Jewish scholar. Amongst other causes of this must be reckoned Abravanel's deep knowledge of Christianity. His bent for eschatology suited his age. English readers will be specially attracted by Abravanel's remarks about the British Isles and their history which Dr Rabinowitz has collected.

Abravanel's views on monarchy and democracy, his agreements with, and his differences from Maimonides in this regard are described by Dr Strauss. The subject will prove of interest to historians and to students of political theory. Dr Strauss examines the relation of Abravanel and his predecessors to Plato and Aristotle.

Finally, Mr Milburn deals with Leone Ebreo, Abravanel's son, and his influence on the Renaissance. This influence was widespread and is severed from its Jewish origin. It has, indeed, been suggested, though on insufficient grounds, that Leone became a Christian. The fact that his *Dialogues* are in the Italian language—though this may not have been their original—made them accessible to a wide circle.

The connection of Abravanel through his son with Renaissance platonism leads on to Spinoza, and so to modern thought. In another direction Abravanel is important to students of Spanish. The great contribution of Spain to European thought is now recognized to have been made in the Middle Ages; and the medieval Spanish thinkers (who were mainly Muslims, or inspired by Muslims) would have had little chance of becoming known in the rest of Europe, if it had not been for the help or translation (as well as the important original contributions) of learned Spanish Jews.

On p. 16 Mr Goodman refers to the expression of thanks recorded by the Senate of Venice and the Council of Ten to Abravanel in connection with his services in concluding the treaty with Portugal. The document was discovered by the late David Kaufmann in the State Archives of Venice and was published by him in the *Revue des Études Juives*, vol. XXXVIII (1899), pp. 145–8. We have thought it desirable to reproduce the text in full in its original form:

MDIII die xii augusti cum additione

Quod domino Isaach Abraha(m)[u]anel hebreo, qui nuper huc venit ex portugallia fecitque eam propositionem in materia spetierum cholocuth quae nunc lecta fuit huic consilio, responderi debeat per capita in hanc sententiam.

Che nuy lo habiamo veduto et aldito voluntieri, si per le bone qualità et virtù de la persona sua, si etiam per la materia proposta, et per la bona mente el dimonstra haver, al beneficio et commodo de la Signoria nostra de la qual el sij cum parolle grave et accommodate rengratiato. Siali deinde facta mention de la antiquissima amicitia et benivolentia, che naturaliter è sempre stata fra quel Ser^{mo}. Re et la Sig^{ria} nostra et tuta la nation portogalese et Venetiana come è noto a tuto il mondo. Poi se subzonzi, che nuy habiamo intesa la oblatione el fa de remandar el suo nepote in portogallo, per portarne una resolutione in questa facenda; et che quando el sara ritornato, nuy aldiremo tuto quello el ne proponerà et ben consyderato et ponderato el tuto, non se partiremo da quelli termini che ne parerano rasonevoli et convenienti. In Caso veramente che la cossa habi luogo, et sortisca effecto, el puol esser certo, che non li è, per manchar la solita gratitudine del stato nostro.

We have made no attempt to reconcile divergent statements of the several lecturers. Such questions as the spelling of the name as Abravanel or Abarbanel are still unsettled. We have followed Baer and Graetz; Dr Gaster, for sound reasons, prefers the latter form. Nor have we eliminated a few repetitions, for these have made each lecture self-contained and have obviated cross-references.

In order to fit this course into the confines of a term the number of weekly lectures had to be limited. The choice of subjects was therefore somewhat restricted. It was, in consequence, impossible to include a consideration of the age of Abravanel and his relation to that age. One of us has added a few remarks on this subject to serve as a general introduction.

It remains for us to express our thanks, and the thanks of our collaborators. First, to those who have made the publication of this volume possible: to the Syndics of the University Press; to the Gentlemen of the Mahamad of the Spanish and Portuguese Jews' Congregation of London; to the Committee of Heshaim; to the Committee of the Endowment of Sir Moses Montefiore, Bart.; and to the Society of Jews and Christians. Secondly, to Mr D. H. Aaron, who has very kindly read the proofs of this book and offered many suggestions of great value.

J. B. TREND
H. LOEWE

6 *December* 1937

ISAAC ABRAVANEL AND HIS AGE

A BRAVANEL's name suggests the meeting point of two epochs, both in Jewish and in general history. During his lifetime we can speak of medievalism fading into modernity. In many respects we stand almost upon the threshold of our own days. There are several tests by which a period may be estimated culturally. Perhaps the simplest is to ask ourselves how we personally should fit into it, and by this means we can judge how much or how little variation has taken place during the intervening years. Thus, most of us would feel more at home during the reign of Queen Anne than under Queen Elizabeth. We prefer the comfort of Wren's houses to the grander architecture of the Tudors: the furniture, costumes, literature and art appeal to us more. Most of all, we would sooner live in an age when we breakfasted off a dish of tea and toast than in an age that started the day with small beer or sack and a haunch of venison.

Now in the age of Abravanel our ancestors had not quite achieved the teapot. But they were well on the way to it, they almost had coffee. It was a fellow-citizen and a contemporary of Isaac, Vasco da Gama, who inaugurated the sea-route to India, and the impetus thus given to oriental commerce made many Eastern rarities familiar to Western households. Coffee[1] was not long in penetrating into Europe. Joseph Caro, who was born in Abravanel's middle age, possibly mentions coffee in the *Shulḥan 'Arukh*. Still, it was not till a century and a half after the death of Abravanel that the berry was first introduced into England by a Jew called Jacob, who, in 1650, opened the first British café in Oxford and thus enriched that city's menu with something besides marmalade.

Therefore when one says that Abravanel lived just on the threshold of modern days, the statement needs precisely that qualification which has been given as an example. Abravanel

---

[1] Coffee from Arabia and Abyssinia came mainly via the Mediterranean but the Eastern trade was, in general, stimulated by the new route.

lived in the days of da Gama the Admiral, not of Jacob the restaurateur. But without the Admiral, the restaurateur would have been impossible. Abravanel never had the pleasure of a good cup of coffee, but in his days people were beginning to long for it. A century and a half before Abravanel represents a much greater cultural remoteness than a century and a half after him. He lived in a time of striving and endeavour, in a time pregnant with far-reaching changes, changes which have directly influenced our own lives, and so with the advent of Abravanel's period we can say that the curtain has been rung down and a new scene is set on the stage.

Let us briefly examine this transformation. Abravanel was born in Lisbon in 1437: he died at Venice in 1508. His life therefore covers an immensely important period in the progress of humanism. Several elements of signal interest contributed to his environment.

First and foremost was the Renaissance. It is usual to date the revival of classical culture from the visit to Italy of Emanuel Chrysoloras in 1396. Emanuel lectured in Florence on Greek literature. Under his stimulus, the desire to read Greek masterpieces arose in Italy and gained strength. The most distinguished men of the day flocked to hear Emanuel, and they carried the seeds of his teaching far and wide. All eyes were turned to Constantinople, whence Emanuel came and whence successors to Emanuel carried on his work. In this revival four periods are usually recognized, and it is worth while to note them. The first was contemporary with the earlier life of Cosimo de' Medici, before he attained power, 1389–1433. During this time the Byzantine scholars were the chief humanists. The second period began in 1433 and lasted until Cosimo's death in 1464. During this period Abravanel was born. The new culture was beginning to spread and was reaching Portugal, faintly perhaps, but surely. Camoens was not born till a dozen years after Abravanel's death. But cultural influences were creeping in. That is to say, although general life in Portugal was scarcely, if at all, affected, yet the intellectuals, to which circle the Abravanel family certainly belonged, were brought under the sway of the Renaissance, and young Isaac grew up in a household where the new learning was discussed. This is clear from his earliest writings, written before the age of 20. These show an acquaintance with contemporary thought that would be hardly explicable if the Abravanel family had lived in literary isolation. What the Renaissance meant for the education of a young man may be gauged from the well-known remark of J. A. Symonds: "English youths who spend their time at Eton between athletic sports and Latin verses and who take an 'Ireland' with a first class in Greats at Oxford, are pursuing the same course of physical and mental discipline as the princes of Gonzaga or Montefeltro in the fifteenth century." Some of these influences must have made themselves felt in the education of Abravanel.

During this second period, an event occurred which reverberated throughout Europe. In 1453, when Isaac was 16, Constantinople fell. The effect of this event on the Renaissance has been variously estimated. But, however low be the estimate, it is safe to say that 1453 must have made a deep impression on young Abravanel and his contemporaries. The Turk was now firmly established in the citadel of the Eastern Empire. Christian dominance suffered a blow in the East which counteracted the triumph in the West, where, nearer to Abravanel's home, the Moors were gradually being expelled from the Iberian peninsula. Thus Abravanel, who saw Christian power ever growing and Islam waning nearer home, was made conscious that the balance was redressed in other quarters, and so, in his youth, he learnt to assess the forces of Islam and Christianity, lessons which were to stand him in good stead, when, later in life, he embraced politics. He never served a Moslem ruler; his political career was spent under four Christian kings. But he never under-valued the force of Islam. The conquest of Constantinople is usually said, though the statement is often contested, to have furthered the revival of learning by releasing the pent-up store of scholarship and by dispersing it over Europe. Exiled scholars fled as refugees to the West, teaching in their new homes and bringing with them precious Greek manuscripts which had escaped the sack of the city. Just so had the overthrow of Bagdad, the Abbassid capital of Islam, led to a revival of Moslem culture two centuries earlier, and just so had the destruction of Jerusalem spread a knowledge of humanism over a wider surface of the globe. The scourge of God does not smite blindly: there is a purpose in the blow. And thus, when Isaac Abravanel was a youth in his most impressionable age, the fall of Constantinople, and the consequences which came from that fall, must have stirred his imagination even as the Great War in our days influenced the brains of those who were old enough to reflect on it but too young to take part in it. In this second period of the Renaissance, while Abravanel was between the ages of 4 and 27, there flourished Fra Lippo Lippi, Sandro Botticelli and Leonardo da Vinci.

The third period of the Renaissance, which synchronized with the opening and ending of the public life of Lorenzo de' Medici (1470–92), coincided with one of the most active portions of Abravanel's life. This was perhaps the most glorious period of the Renaissance. Education was revolutionized and the foundations of accurate scholarship were laid.

The last period of the Renaissance (1492–1527) reaches 19 years beyond the life of Abravanel and ends with the sack of Rome during the pontificate of the Medicean Pope Clement VII. Henceforth Rome supplanted Florence. It was the age of Michael Angelo, Andrea del Sarto and Raphael. The Renaissance spent itself in different ways in different lands. In Holland and Italy it found expression chiefly in art, in England in literature and in Spain and Portugal in exploration, literature and colonization. The Renaissance, then, was the first important element that must be taken into account in visualizing the environment in which Abravanel lived.

The second element is the invention of printing. In the year after the fall of Constantinople, that is to say in 1454, when Abravanel was 17 years old, the earliest dated documents printed from movable type appeared in Mainz, from the founts of Fust and Gutenberg. A stroll through the galleries of the King's Library in the British Museum brings home with remarkable clarity the relative progress made by the new art in the various countries of Europe, for the visitor will there see a series of show-cases in which specimens of *incunabula* are grouped geographically. The case devoted to Portugal reveals the significant fact that the first press in that country was established by Jews and that in 1495, when Portugal contained five presses, three were Jewish and produced Hebrew books. It was at Faro, in 1487, that the first Hebrew book in Portugal was printed. At that time Abravanel had been for four years an exile from his native land. He was already fifty years old but his youth had passed during the infancy of typography. If we think of the inventions of our own day of motors and submarines and wireless and X-rays, we shall have a faint, but only a faint, vision of the age of Abravanel, for how can these things, wonderful as they indeed are, compare in importance to mankind with the wonder of the printing press? Now, for the first time, literature was placed in the grasp of the many. Books were multiplied, learning was facilitated. Mankind was stirring from the torpor of the dark ages and at this juncture Abravanel lived. To us the spate of books which floods our shelves is a commonplace that arouses no thrill but we can picture to ourselves the excitement that must have sped far and wide when rumours circulated that, at long last, this or that masterpiece of antiquity, this or that much coveted poem or history or commentary was brought within reach of the eager reader. To this delight Isaac could look forward and his father must no doubt frequently have pointed out to him the immense contrast between the days of old and the present. And so, in considering Isaac's environment, we must take into account that he lived in a time when the private library was a possibility within the powers of the middle classes, not the cherished monopoly of the wealthy nobility.

The third factor of importance in the environment of Abravanel is largely the outcome of the two former. The Renaissance and the printing press created thought and thought demanded intellectual freedom, liberty to think as reason demanded and liberty to worship as conscience required. The result of these tendencies was the Reformation.

Now the actual Reformation belongs to a later period. It was in 1517, nine years after Abravanel was buried, that Martin Luther startled the world by publishing his famous theses in which he attacked the sale of indulgences. But during the lifetime of Abravanel the pot was seething though it was not till after his death that it boiled over. Two hundred years had elapsed since the Albigenses had vainly attempted to challenge the supremacy of the Church. In the fourteenth and fifteenth centuries the renewed demand for internal reform was successfully resisted. The Lollards were suppressed in England, John Huss, the Bohemian disciple of Wycliffe, was put to death at Constance in 1415, 22 years before the birth of Abravanel, and the Hussites, after many victories, were defeated. In Basle the Reforming party were unable to carry through the proposed changes in the organization of the Church. But postponement and hesitation hampered the efforts of the Papacy. Discontent became the more powerful the more it was checked and disappointment and delay gave time for the development of new forces in which religious malcontents were to find powerful allies. The Renaissance destroyed the clerical monopoly of learning and education and brought with it a questioning and a critical spirit which could not be excluded from the domain of religion. Above all, the growing force of national consciousness inspired a spirit of revolt against the domination and the pecuniary exactions of an alien spiritual authority. It is often said that at the beginning of the fifteenth century, it might have been possible to reform the worst abuses of the Church and yet retain its unity and cohesion. By the beginning of the sixteenth century this was no longer possible. During this period of ferment, when men were speaking and thinking and writing and acting so much and so vehemently on the subject of religion, Abravanel lived and died. Moreover he lived in a stronghold of Catholicism and this had an important influence on his pen. Had his life been spent in closer contact with the Reformers, had his days been spared the horrors of the Inquisition, which was reorganized in Spain in 1478, Abravanel's views of Christianity might have been very different, wide though they were. What this difference would have been we can gauge by comparing Abravanel's views with those of his younger contemporary, Elijah Levita, who was born in 1468 and who lived on terms of intimacy and friendship with Protestant as well as Catholic divines, with Paulus Fagius as well as Cardinal Egidio of Viterbo. But Abravanel's years coincided with the years of preparation for freedom and he died in the blackest period of darkness, just before the dawn.

The fourth element that claims consideration is geographical. We have mentioned the developments of the intellect that belong to the age of Abravanel, there remains the development of the material side, territorial expansion. This is particularly important in the case of Abravanel because he was a Portuguese and in the Iberian peninsula, where Catholicism was so firmly entrenched, the spirit of the Renaissance found its outlet in maritime adventure. Spain and Portugal sent out pioneers whose heroism enlarged the bounds of the habitable globe and it was during the lifetime of Abravanel that this stupendous advance was made. In 1492 Christopher Columbus, who was but two years older than Abravanel, set sail on his momentous voyage that resulted in the discovery of America. In 1498, Vasco da Gama, from Portugal, who was 32 years younger than his fellow-citizen Abravanel, reached India by the sea-route. As will be seen, Abravanel was at one time occupied in the political consequences of the latter discovery. It needs but little imagination to picture the effect which the work of da Gama and Columbus must have exercised on their contemporaries. This one factor alone would suffice to draw this period into close relation with our own. When we sum up the foregoing and reflect that Abravanel lived in a time of printed books, of intellectual and religious emancipation, of a world enlarged by the inclusion of America and India, we must acknowledge that we are in all truth standing on the threshold of our own days and that Abravanel is almost to be considered as a child of our own age.

So much for the general environment in which Abravanel is to be placed. Now what of the Jewish surroundings? Abravanel comes between Maimonides and the *Shulḥan 'Arukh*, of which the author, Joseph Caro, was born in 1488, when Abravanel was at the height of his fame. Let us take the four factors that we considered in the creation of the general environment and apply them to the Judaism in which Abravanel is to be set. By the end of the Middle Ages the Jews had been politically and socially degraded in many lands, not, however, in Spain and Portugal. But though the Jews were crushed externally, the Ghetto was, to a large extent, free from the tyranny internally. That is to say, within the Ghetto there was light. True, the period was not one of great literary brilliance. Scientific labours were laid aside, the shadow of Montpellier, where Jewish obscurantists had banned the learning of Maimonides and declared his spirit to be incompatible with Judaism, still hung over Jewries. But contrasted with the larger world without, Jewry was intellectually advanced. It was an age of *Pilpul* (scholastic dialectics) rather than an age of philosophy and poetry but this generalization is very hazardous and corrective details, for which there is no space here, would somewhat modify the picture. But just because Judaism was not so backward as the environment, the reaction was slower. The effect of the Renaissance was more gradual, just for the very reason that there was not so much lost ground to be made up. Printing was welcomed by the Jews. They termed it *Melékheth haḳ-Ḳódesh*, the holy work. Books were being printed in amazing numbers, not only in Hebrew but in Judaeo-German and in other dialects. Not long after Caxton began to popularize romances, Jewish presses were turning out cheap books for the use of the people, love poems, secular stories, fables and histories, as well as books of piety, Holy Scriptures and liturgies. The share of the Jews in exploration has often been told. In the late fifteenth and early sixteenth centuries Jewish travellers abounded. In 1501 a Seville Jewess was in India, making the grand tour in the platonic company of two Christian gentlemen. When Vasco da Gama reached India, a Jew from Posen was there to meet him and tried to capture his fleet single-handed. The news of the route to India was brought to Portugal by two

Jews in the service of the Portuguese king, Abraham of Beja and Joseph of Lamego. One of them was a cobbler and it is fascinating to reflect that the first reports of the wealth of the Indies were brought to their future owners by a poor Jewish shoemaker. Similarly Columbus was indebted to Abraham Zacuto for the maps and instruments of navigation that rendered his voyage possible. All these events occurred in the lifetime of Abravanel. From this meagre outline it is possible to realise that he lived in an age of vigour and effort and that in this *Drang nach Osten* the Jews took a fair share, far more than the restrictions on their movement would, one might imagine, have permitted.

In Portugal the earlier kings had protected the Jews but had compelled them to live in *juderías*, or Jewish quarters. Ever since 1223, the Jewish courts enjoyed autonomy in civil and criminal jurisdiction: the Chief Rabbi was appointed by the king and was entitled to use the royal arms on his seal. In 1443 Alphonso V ascended the throne. This monarch, who reigned till 1481 and was one of the best that ever reigned in the land, was noted for his gentle character. Among his noteworthy acts was his offering an asylum to the exiles from Constantinople. Alphonso permitted his Jewish subjects to live outside the *juderías* and relieved them from the obligation of wearing a distinctive costume, an ordinance enforced since 1325. During his reign, says the *Shevet Yehudah* of Solomon ibn Virga, the Jews enjoyed freedom and prospered. It was their last tranquil period in the peninsula. Alphonso promoted Jews to public offices and admitted them to his friendship. In culture the Jews far surpassed the Christians of Portugal. The Jews were well versed in the philosophy of Aristotle and in scholastic studies; in Astronomy, Science and Medicine they occupied a very high rank. They furnished several royal physicians. They were pioneers and intelligencers. In commerce they were especially prominent, indeed the expulsion of the Jews ruined Portuguese trade. They prospered in business, in spite of the fact that Jews paid special taxes on practically every transaction, besides a special poll tax of 30 *dinheiros* in memory of the 30 pieces of silver paid to Judas

Iscariot. For this reason, they were naturally favoured by the crown. For centuries they lived on good terms with the commons and the subsequent prejudice that was stirred up against them was due partly, no doubt, to injudicious ostentation on the Jewish side but far more to the deliberate action of the Clergy and the nobles, but this prejudice was neither innate in the populace nor fostered by the king; nor were most Jews ostentatious. As often happens, the many suffer for the folly of a few.

We may now turn to the biographical facts of Isaac Abravanel. The name is spelled Abarbanel and Abravanel. Elias Levita, a contemporary of Isaac, calls him אַבַּרבִּינָאל, but the evidence of a contemporary is not always decisive, as analogies from Pepys and others show. Nor is the meaning of the name known. Most probably is it to be derived from a place. The family was a distinguished one. Isaac, in the introduction to his commentary on Isaiah, claimed descent from David. According to the *Sheveṭ Yehudah* there were other families of this pedigree in Spain also; Isaac ibn Ghayyath also laid claim to royal lineage. Judah Abravanel dwelt in Seville: his grandson, Samuel, settled at Valencia. He and his son Judah emigrated to Portugal where, about 1400, he became the king's treasurer at Lisbon. He also managed the financial affairs of prince Fernando, who, in 1437, assigned to him over half a million *reis blancos*. In that year Isaac, the subject of these lectures, was born. In consequence of his father's intellectual ability and position at court, Isaac received a first class secular education: he was equally well instructed in Jewish matters by Joseph Ḥayyim, the Lisbon Rabbi. He specialized in philosophy. In Lisbon the first period of his life, extending to 44 years, was spent. Before he was 20 years of age he had written on natural science and given evidence of marked ability. At the age of 20 he composed his first book, *'Aṭéreth Zeḳenim*, and he also began to lecture on the book of Deuteronomy in the Synagogue but the manuscript was mislaid and published only after an interval of many years. But during this first period of his life his literary activities were interrupted by other pursuits. He sketched and planned books which he completed in subsequent years. Now he was busied mainly with politics and philanthropy. His agile brain soon attracted notice and he, in his turn, was appointed to his father's post and became the royal treasurer. In this position he achieved remarkable success and enjoyed the favour and friendship of Alphonso V. All this time he exerted himself on behalf of the Jews. As a result of a war in Morocco many Jews were enslaved and Abravanel set himself to buy them out of servitude. But his efforts were soon needed nearer home. The Jews incurred the envy of the populace owing to the favour shown them by the king. For the first time in Portugal an attack on the Jews broke out and in 1449 the *judería* in Lisbon was sacked by the mob. Several Jews were killed. The king interfered on their behalf. With Abravanel's help the sufferers were relieved and the miscreants punished. At the Assemblies of the Cortes at Santarem in 1451, at Lisbon in 1455, at Coimbra in 1473, restrictions against the Jews were demanded by the representatives of the people and refused by the king. Again at Evora, in 1481, the same requests were put forward. In that year Alphonso V died, and, as Abravanel says, "all Israel was filled with grief and mourning: the people fasted and wept". Alphonso was succeeded by his son John II, who was of a morose disposition and not like his father. So far as the Jews were concerned, the policy of the previous reign was not changed. John showed them favour in numerous ways but of this nothing need now be said because the first period of Abravanel's life is now drawing to a close and in the second he was not in Portugal. Therefore he was not directly affected by the fate of the Portuguese Jews. John's political policy was directed against the nobles who had long been in opposition to the crown. John, on his accession declared that the liberality of former kings had left the crown no estates save the high roads of Portugal and he determined to crush the feudal nobility and seize its territories. A Cortes held at Evora in 1481, which proposed restrictions on the Jews, also empowered judges nominated by the crown to administer justice in all feudal domains. The nobles resisted this infringement of their rights but their leader, Ferdinand, Duke of Braganza, was beheaded for high treason in 1483. The king stabbed to death his own brother-in-law, the Duke of Vizeu, and 80 other members of the aristocracy were executed. Thus John, the perfect, as he was called, assured the supremacy of the crown. And Abravanel? His enemies persuaded the king that he was supporting the Duke of Braganza and John gave orders for Abravanel's arrest. His condemnation would have been certain but he received timely warning and made his escape. He fled to Castile and thus, in 1483, the first period of his career came to an end. In later years, when he wrote his commentary to the Book of Kings, he referred to this period as the happiest in his life. He was one of the richest Jews of Portugal and his house was a focus of all the learned world, Jewish and non-Jewish. Among these was certainly included the Duke of Braganza, but there is no evidence that Abravanel had any complicity in his political schemes. And now he was a penniless fugitive, for all his vast fortune was confiscated by the king. He reached Castile with his life and nothing else.

From the frontier Abravanel wrote to the king an impassioned letter protesting his innocence. But this was of no avail. On hearing that his property had been sequestrated, Abravanel continued his journey. He settled in Toledo, where he was followed by his wife and his sons Joseph and Samuel. Judah, another son, remained in Portugal.

The second chapter of his life, the Spanish period, now opens and this lasted till 1492. On his arrival at Toledo Abravanel resumed his literary activity. He had contemplated a commentary on the prophets and in a very short time he completed three books. He must have been a quick worker, judging by the time spent on his task, and it must moreover be remembered that Abravanel is rather diffuse in style. At all events the commentary on Joshua was finished in 16 days, that on Judges in 24 days, and that on Samuel in 75 days. He now began a commentary on Kings but politics intervened. So great was his fame that he was summoned to enter the service of the Spanish crown. He farmed the revenues and refilled the depleted exchequer and supplied the army with provisions. Abravanel rose high in the royal favour and was often able to protect his brethren from the attacks of the Inquisition. But the sands were running out. Torquemada's agitation had its effect and in 1492 the blow fell. The decree of banishment which was launched against the Spanish Jews and which Abravanel did his best to prevent need not have applied to Abravanel, for the king offered to let him remain. But Abravanel accompanied his brethren.

The third chapter in Abravanel's life now opens. Just three months before Columbus set sail for his discovery of America, Abravanel left Spain with his family and betook himself with his household to Naples. The first thing he did was to get to work on his interrupted commentary on the book of Kings and this he finished, with his accustomed rapidity, by the eve of the Jewish New Year in 1493. But just as in his exile from Portugal he was not suffered to remain long in private life, so here too, in Naples, his reputation reached the ears of the king. Ferdinand of Naples, unlike his contemporary namesake of Spain, was a humane monarch and a wise one. He welcomed the Jews and he employed Abravanel. Ferdinand was threatened with war by the French and he needed all the aid he could gather in making his preparations. So once again Abravanel entered royal service. Ferdinand was succeeded by his son Alphonso II who retained Abravanel in his service. In January 1494 the French king Charles VIII conquered Naples. Abravanel's house was plundered and his valuable library destroyed, after it had survived the vicissitudes of the emigration from Spain. Abravanel went into exile yet again, following his prince Alphonso to Messina in 1495. Alphonso died in June of that year. During this period, in addition to the commentary on Kings, Abravanel wrote a book called *Rosh 'Amanah* in which he explained the fundamental principles of Judaism and criticised the Thirteen Articles of the Creed of Maimonides. He also began his commentary on the later prophets.

Hitherto the family of Abravanel had been united. The conquest of Naples dispersed them. The most tragic fate of all overtook his eldest son Judah Leon Medigo, who was born in 1470. Judah was kept in Spain as a Marrano. His little son Isaac was to be detained as a hostage, to prevent Judah from quitting the country. Judah, hearing of this, smuggled his son away to Portugal but thought it safer not to go with him, so he went to Naples. But John II seized young Isaac Abravanel and had him baptized. Isaac never saw his parents again. He was brought up as a Christian. The agony of the father at the living death of his lost son was boundless. But thousands of parents were in a similar plight, by reason of the wholesale abduction of Jewish children at the bidding of the Inquisition, and their forcible baptism.

After the death of Alphonso II in 1495, Abravanel went to Corfu. Here he began his commentary on Isaiah but this took him 3 years to complete. When the French in 1496 evacuated the kingdom of Naples, Abravanel returned and settled at Monopoli. He was separated from his wife and children and sought alleviation in writing. To this period belong several of his books, all of which need not now be specified. Mention must be made, however, of his famous commentary on the Passover *Haggadah* and of the works he wrote in defence of Judaism against Christianity. This task he undertook on behalf of the Marranos and also to strengthen the faith of those Jews who were constantly subject to the arguments of the Missionaries. In 1508 Abravanel died in Venice and was buried in Padua. In consequence of the spoliation of the country, his grave is unknown.

So ended the career of a truly remarkable man. Just consider the stirring days in which his life was cast. Here was a man who lived through the Renaissance, the invention of printing, the fall of Constantinople, the birth-pangs of the Reformation, the discovery of America and the opening of the sea route to India. In the compass of 71 years he witnessed all these significant events, but fate prevented him from enjoying them to the full. Christopher Columbus set sail for America on August 3, 1492; the mass of the Spanish Jews wandered forth into exile on the previous day, which was appropriately enough, the ninth Ab, the fast day commemorating the fall of the two Temples. Again, Vasco da Gama left Lisbon in 1499; Abravanel, the chief man in the kingdom was there no more: he had long been driven out, a fugitive. In 1487 the first book, a Hebrew book too, was printed in Portugal, but again Abravanel was not suffered by fortune to be present at this epoch-making occasion. He suffered exile three times and was forced to be a wanderer till his old age. He died sundered from wife and children. His life may be regarded as typical of that of his people and it is significant that he should have written so much about the Messiah. He laid the greatest stress on the doctrine of the gradual development of mankind to a better knowledge of God and a better relation between man and man. He looked ahead. Evil and persecution were transitory and would give way to good. Israel has been called the "suffering servant" and if ever the character of the Messiah in Isaiah LII–LIII can be capable of a personal application, surely it is to Abravanel that it may be applied—Abravanel, the man of sorrows and acquainted with grief, at whom kings shut their mouths and who suffered the sinfulness of many. Yet it would be a great error to depict the life of Abravanel as continuously unfortunate. This is a mistake to which Jewish writers are prone, a mistake too often repeated in Jewish history generally. Misfortunes indeed he suffered. But there were long periods of quiet and happiness in his life. Of his 71 years, we must certainly exclude the first 44, which he himself declared to be supremely peaceful and blessed. In the second period he must likewise have had 6 or 7 years unclouded by trouble, and later on there were, similarly, bright times amid the gloom. When we examine a biography or when we cast a glance at history, we often ignore the normal. We fix our eyes on the noteworthy events and overlook the commonplace days. Yet these are, in truth, the happy ones. Happy is the people that has no history. Let us look at our own lives. If we were to keep a diary, we should certainly note down the outstanding events. We should record births and marriages and we should include deaths, worries, illnesses, losses in business, opportunities missed, hopes frustrated and bitter disappointments. But we should not put down our average day's programme, our dull and uneventful occupations that constitute our quiet existence. Yet this is life. Not the exceptional and not the bizarre. In fact, if we truly analyse our time we shall find that no inconsiderable portion of it, possibly one third to one half of our entire life, is spent in bed.

Why do we consider Abravanel a great man? Is it because he was the last Jewish Aristotelian? Scarcely. The world is not troubled now with the controversy whether matter is or is not eternal. That is a relatively minor point. The fact is that of Abravanel we may say as we do of Maimonides that though his methods may be obsolete yet his spirit and his system have permanent value. We can still and for long learn from them. Nor is the fact that Abravanel wrote over twenty books in itself enough to command our interest in him. Others have written more volumes, which repose unread on library shelves. The great things about Abravanel were his sanity and dignity. In his books, he was often imaginative and even fantastic. In his actions he was sober and deliberate. He never lost his head; he never exaggerated; he took long views; he had a calm and judicial outlook. How many of us, over-whelmed by gigantic catastrophes, time after time, would have recovered our balance! How many of us would have made a fresh start after experiencing calamities such as those which relentlessly pursued Abravanel! How many of us would have shone as a leader in such terrible days as 1492, when a whole people was driven out into exile and needed aid and counsel and calm guidance to save them from frenzied despair! In all the chaos of the flight from Spain Abravanel stood firm as a rock. He never "despaired of the State" and amid the overwhelming attacks of Church and Crown he was able to prepare a double defence, to organize the relief of the wanderers and to fit them out with literary weapons with which to meet their adversaries who sought to destroy their faith in their religion.

Why was Abravanel so successful? Why were his books read and re-read by Jews? Why were his defence of Judaism and his criticisms of Christianity so carefully considered and deemed so serious by numerous Christian scholars? Not only

on account of his learning, not merely because of his modera-
tion, but also for the reason that Abravanel was a master of
general scholarship. He knew the arguments of Christian
scholars. Not only could he meet them on their own ground
but he could evaluate their work and use the valuable residue
for teaching Jews. He was steeped in the humanities, as well
as in Jewish lore, and so he could frame a reasoned verdict and
his pleas carried conviction.

Abravanel was a true *Shtadlan* (Defender), always to the
fore in the defence of his brethren. But there have been
others. Why was he distinguished from them? Because, in
addition to being a wealthy man, an influential man, an
inordinately charitable man and a conspicuous philanthropist,
he was also a scholar and an amateur scholar. Today we do
not combine the roles. We have scholars, we have philanthro-
pists, we have *Shtadlanim* (Defenders), but are the parts united?

The man who put the finances of three kingdoms into
order, the man who managed the taxation of a nation and
refilled the depleted exchequer without exactions, the man
who successfully provided the supplies for an army across the
seas was essentially a man of affairs and at the same time he
was a philosopher and an exegete. And his faith in God
never wavered.

H. LOEWE.

DON ISAAC ABRAVANEL

Lecture I

INTRODUCTION

BY PAUL GOODMAN

INTRODUCTION[1]

DON ISAAC ABRAVANEL lived at a time which proved decisive in the development of European civilization, and he was not only the last of the galaxy of great Jews on the soil of Sepharad (Spain), but he participated actively in the events of his age. As a youth of eighteen, he heard of the capture of Constantinople by the Turks, resulting in the flight of the scholars of Byzantium, who, by their dispersal far and wide, brought about the period of the Renaissance. The discovery of printing gave the impetus to a cultural upheaval of incomparable consequence. The quest for the sea route to India by the venturers of Spain and Portugal and the discovery of America by Christopher Columbus in the fateful year 1492 brought into being a new world which was to redress the balance of the old. Unlimited economic and social potentialities, as far-reaching as the technical developments of to-day, then presented themselves for the weal and woe of mankind.

The epoch in which Isaac Abravanel lived was also one of the most tragic in the chequered annals of the Jewish people. More than in any other part of their Dispersion, the Jews on the Iberian peninsula have acquired immortal renown both by their achievements and by their martyrdom. Moorish-Jewish co-operation built a bridge over the Middle Ages between the ancient world and the new. The Jews and crypto-Jews shared in the discoveries and in the economic development or exploitation of the infinitely vast acquisitions by Spain and Portugal. To these Jews, known as Sephardim, the names of the cities of Toledo and Cordova, Granada and Seville, acquired a significance, proud and sad beyond compare. There stands Lisbon, built upon towering hills with the view of a bay rare in its beauty, which has immemorial Semitic associations with the Jews and their Phoenician cousins and fellow-traders. Even to-day, the

[1] This Address was delivered originally in German at a Commemoration of Don Isaac Abravanel at the Great Hall of the University of Tartu (Dorpat), Esthonia, on 17 April 1937 (see Preface, p. viii).

attention of the visitor is still attracted by the Semitic phy-
siognomy of many of the inhabitants, particularly by the
graceful figures of the Ovarinas, the female fish vendors of
Carthaginian origin, that are to be seen in their archaic
attire in the steep and narrow lanes of the poorer quarters of
Lisbon.

It was in this capital city of Portugal that five hundred
years ago there was born a scion of the Jewish race who may
be designated as the last of the great Jews of the Middle
Ages. Don Isaac Abravanel, statesman and financier, philosopher and Bible commentator, a Jew true to his ancestral
faith and devoted to the last to his people—thus has he
remained a unique figure in history. He represents the
Sephardi Jew at his best; in him was incorporated in an exceptional measure תורה וגדולה במקום אחד, the union of
Torah and social distinction.

Don Isaac Abravanel claimed descent from the royal house
of David. According to the family tradition, his forbears
came to Spain after the destruction of the first Temple in
Jerusalem and settled in Seville. It is on record that an
Abravanel was in Seville in the year 1310. Don Jhuda
Abravaniel, as he was called, was *almoxarife*, a Royal
Treasurer, and exercised such influence at Court that Don
Isaac applied to him and his descendants the biblical verse
(Gen. XLIX, 10): "The Sceptre shall not depart from Judah,
nor a lawgiver from between his feet." Don Isaac appears
to have been fully convinced of his Davidic origin, for in his
commentaries on books of the Scriptures he thus describes
himself:

אני הגבר יצחק בן איש חי רב פעלים בישראל גדול שמו
אדון יהודה בן שמואל בן יהודה...מבני אברבנאל כלם אנשים
ראשי בני ישראל משורש ישי בית הלחמי ממשפחת בית
דוד נגיד ומצוה לאומי ז"צל ·

("I, Isaac, son of. . .Judah, son of Samuel, son of Judah. . .of
the stock of Jesse the Bethlehemite. . . .")

In any case, there is no doubt that his patrician forbears had rendered valuable services to the State and to their people. His grandfather, Don Samuel, was a financier of importance under Henry II of Trastamara (1369–79), but, having been forced after the death of the King to adopt Christianity under the name of Juan Sanches de Sevilla, he settled in Lisbon in order to be able to return openly to his ancestral religion. His son Judah, the father of Don Isaac, acquired a considerable influence at the Portuguese Court, especially as treasurer of the Infante Dom Fernando, the brother of King Duarte of Portugal.

Isaac Abravanel enjoyed a careful education, which was not confined to traditional Jewish studies but extended to classical literature and the general culture of his time. In addition to a remarkably thorough knowledge of the Bible he possessed an extensive acquaintance with the works of Jewish and Christian exegetes, with Talmudical literature and the writings of medieval poets and philosophers. Besides the many quotations from Latin commentaries of Christian theologians which appear in his works, there is ascribed to him the translation of Thomas Aquinas' treatise *Quaestio de spiritualibus creaturis* (the manuscript of which was in the possession of Moses Almosnino in the sixteenth century). He was acquainted with Arabic and possibly also with Greek. His daily language was Portuguese, which he used, not only on account of his environment or habit, but by reason of the profound attachment to that tongue which Jews of Portuguese origin have manifested for centuries after their exile—just as so many groups of Spanish Jews have retained the language of Castile to this day. Later he acquired a literary knowledge of Spanish and Italian. Although at first he was not able to handle Hebrew with great fluency, he later on used it in his literary work by preference with exceptional skill and elegance.

He was a man of the world and had acquired a range of knowledge unusual in its width, and, by journeys he had undertaken abroad for business purposes, was acquainted with the customs and political conditions prevailing in foreign lands.

Don Isaac Abravanel was destined to occupy a high position in the service of his native country and to enjoy there a high social status, for members of his family had for generations been entrusted by kings and noblemen with the conduct of their finances and had stood in close relationship to them. His own personal inclinations and talents paved the way to a leading role in the financial affairs of the Portuguese State. He thus occupied an influential position as treasurer at the Court of King Alfonso V (1438–81), and was on particularly confidential terms with Fernando, Duke of Braganza, one of the most powerful nobles in the kingdom. Alfonso, who, until his death, remained well disposed to Don Isaac, granted him an estate at Queluz. He was exempted from the obligation, imposed on other Jews, of wearing the badge, and was given the right, then denied to them, of riding on a mule.

Don Isaac, in the introduction to his commentary on the book of Joshua, thus describes the position he had enjoyed:

Happy was I in the palace of Don Alfonso, the powerful king, whose dominion extended over two seas, the king who sat on the throne of justice, who exercised mercy and ruled with righteousness in the land. He had eaten of the tree of knowledge and possessed grace and understanding....While his riches grew, God remembered his people. Relief and deliverance arose to the Jews. Under his shadow I loved to dwell. I stood near to him and he leant on my hand. And so long as he lived on earth I walked in the royal palace.

It was through the relations of King Alfonso with the Signoria of Florence and the Medici that Abravanel was, presumably, able to get into communication with Italian authorities, and his correspondence with the Florentine banker and Maecenas, Jehiel of Pisa, was strengthened by the visit to the latter of the physician João Sezira, a friend of Abravanel, who, on a mission from King Alfonso to Rome, also carried with him a petition by Abravanel to Pope Sixtus IV, on matters affecting the Jews.

Isaac Abravanel was a leader of the Jewish Community of Lisbon, and one of the interesting features of his activities, described in a communication by him to Jehiel of Pisa, was the manumission of 250 Jewish captives who fell into the hands of the Portuguese, on the conquest of Arzilla, in Morocco. The efforts which he devoted to this purpose is a magnificent example of the *Mizvah* of *Pidyon Shebuim* (duty of redemption of captives) as it was carried out by Jews at that time.

Abravanel was the possessor of a great fortune, which he had partly inherited from his ancestors but which he owed largely to his own enterprise. The extent of his wealth was particularly manifested by the fact that he contributed a tenth part of the indemnity imposed on Portugal after the unfortunate issue of the war with Castile. But these circumstances came to a sudden end with the death of King Alfonso in the year 1481. John II, who changed entirely the policy pursued by his father, accused Abravanel of a conspiracy against the King with Duke Fernando of Braganza, who was executed in 1483, and, although Abravanel protested his innocence, he could save himself only by flight to neighbouring Castile. But all his possessions were confiscated, and he, together with his son-in-law Joseph Abravanel, were subsequently condemned to death *in contumacia*.

Thus, in his forty-eighth year, Don Isaac Abravanel had to begin his life anew. By the part he played in Portuguese finances, he established influential contact with the rulers of Spain, who came to value and utilize his great experience in financial affairs. It is only thus that it is possible to explain his remarkable change from the position of an exile deprived of his fortune to that of a trusted adviser of the Catholic Ferdinand and Isabella. In 1484 King Ferdinand entrusted him with the financial administration of the country, and retained Abravanel's services until the hapless year 1492. In this position, Abravanel was, during the course of eight years, called upon to provide the financial resources for the pursuit of the war against Granada, the last Moorish stronghold on Spanish soil. Jointly with the Court Rabbi and chief tax-farmer Abraham Senior, he supplied the army with provisions, and rendered particularly valuable services to the country by applying not only his own wealth for that purpose but by inducing other Jews to follow his example.

Of exceptional historic interest is the meeting of Abravanel with Christopher Columbus at Malaga in August 1487. According to M. Kayserling, it may be assumed that they had already met in Lisbon, where Columbus had had dealings with a number of Jews, and that Abravanel was the first to afford financial support to Columbus' undertaking. But the part which Isaac Abravanel played in the Pyrenean peninsula came to a tragic end in 1492 on the expulsion of the Jews by Ferdinand and Isabella from Spanish soil.

This event has remained unique in its immeasurable cruelty, as it does in the martyrdom of the exiles. We stand amazed and deeply moved before this noble and unexampled confession of faith. Proud in their bearing and steadfast in their faith, these Spanish Jews departed from the land which they had enriched and made renowned by their spirit and their energies. On the fast-day of the Ninth of Ab—commemorating the twofold destruction of the Temple of Jerusalem—these Spanish Jews left their native country for ever. In the words of Isaac Abravanel:

Their King went before them, their fear of God and their love for Him. They did not blaspheme, nor did they desecrate His Covenant; they left in the anguish and shame of their widowhood. And they moved from people to people, hither and thither, fugitives and wanderers, until they disappeared from the face of the earth.

We, here, who are now living four and a half centuries after this terror, know the verdict of history, the judgement which it has passed on the persecutors and the persecuted.

Not all the Jews departed. There remained behind the eighty-years-old Abraham Senior, who was closely connected with Isaac Abravanel in their financial transactions; and as this venerable Rabbi and courtier stood at the baptismal font, there were at his side the King and Queen as his sponsors.

Isaac Abravanel went into exile. On three occasions he implored the rulers of the country to withdraw the dread edict. He offered 30,000 gold ducats. And as he had almost succeeded in his efforts, the Grand Inquisitor Thomas Torquemada, the father confessor of the Queen, is said to have appeared before the royal couple, crucifix in hand, with the dramatic appeal: "Behold Him, whom Judas sold for thirty pieces of silver, and whom ye would sell now for 30,000!"[1]

The order of expulsion became irrevocable. Yet for decades, nay for centuries, Jewish neo-Christians remained in the country of their birth, and the Spanish sky was reddened by the fires of the stakes whereby in *autos-da-fé* the spiritual nostalgia of men and women of Jewish blood was to be exterminated.

Isaac Abravanel was fifty-four years old when he left Spain for Italy with his three sons, Judah, Joseph and Samuel. The Spanish Government considered it opportune to retain relations with this very important Jewish family for the future. The authorities took over a substantial part of the Abravanel properties and mitigated the rigours which were generally applied to the Jewish exiles. At first, Abravanel stayed in Naples; he then had to escape to Sicily and afterwards fled to Corfu. He remained for some time at Monopoli, on the coast of Apulia; and then went to Venice, where he died in his seventy-first year, on 25 November 1508. His mortal remains were interred in Padua; but this city was sacked a year afterwards, and the grave of one of the noblest sons of the Jewish people has remained unknown to this day.

Isaac Abravanel's eldest son, Judah, was born about 1460. Judah, who settled with his father in Italy and, under the name of Leone Ebreo, became renowned by his *Dialoghi di Amore*, was a physician by profession. He practised medicine before his departure from Lisbon in 1483, and acquired distinction on his settlement in Castile. Among the children of the exiles from Spain who found refuge in Portugal was Judah's little son—named Isaac after his grandfather—a child one year old. King Ferdinand, who had a high regard for Judah Abravanel's medical skill, endeavoured to persuade him to accept the Christian faith, and, on failing in this

[1] This scene forms the subject of a famous picture by S. Hart, R.A.

attempt, secretly directed the boy to be baptized. This, however, came to the knowledge of the father, who sent the child in charge of a nurse to relations in Portugal so that his son might eventually join him in Italy. The measures which King John II of Portugal took to subject Jewish children forcibly to baptism affected also the young Isaac Abravanel, and, as was the fate of innumerable other Jewish children at that time, this scion of the Abravanel family disappeared in the cataclysm which then engulfed the exiles of Sepharad.

The vicissitudes of Don Isaac Abravanel at the Courts of the Christian Kings in Portugal, Spain and Italy represent a very remarkable phenomenon: intensely Jewish though he was, he moved, conscious of his noble Jewish lineage, freely and with an apparently self-assured dignity in an atmosphere that was so impregnated with the mystical glamour and impelled by the temporal might of the Universal Church that it could not tolerate any other religious manifestation. There was, indeed, a *Judería*, but without the cramping effect of the ghetto or *Judengasse* of Central and Eastern Europe. The Sephardi Jews were not aliens, living apart from the autochthonous people of the land, but were by their language, mentality and mode of life an almost indistinguishable part of the general landscape. Their mental equipment fitted in well with their intellectual environment. In Poland, the Jews also felt at home, not only religiously but intellectually, yet there was an insurmountable barrier between them and their Catholic neighbours. Quite otherwise was the relationship between Jew and Christian on the Iberian peninsula when fanaticism was not stirred to frenzy. For instance, in the case of Solomon ibn Gabirol, there was not the slightest trace of Jewish authorship in his philosophical work *Meḳor Ḥaim* (*Fons Vitæ*[1]). In striking contrast to the cramped intellectual horizon of the

---

[1] "And so, for centuries Gabirol marched through the philosophic schools of medieval Europe, some taking him for a Christian and some for a Mohammedan, none suspecting that he was a Jew. It was on November 12, 1846, that the learned world was startled by the announcement of Solomon Munk, in the *Literaturblatt des Orients*, that the well-known scholastic Avicebron was identical with the still better known Solomon ibn Gabirol." (I. Davidson, *Selected Religious Poems of Solomon ibn Gabirol*, Philadelphia, 1923, p. xxxii.)

Jewish religious teachers in other parts, the Jews of Sephardi origin possessed an extraordinarily wide outlook and acquaintance with the outer, non-Jewish world. This showed itself to an exceptional degree in a *Universalgenie* like Moses Maimonides, but even in men of lesser stature we find a refreshing association of secular learning and worldly wisdom with traditional Jewish faith and piety. Long after their exile from the lands whose names they still bore with a pride that was innate and which in many instances they adorned, this felicitous synthesis of Hispano-Jewish culture was retained and cultivated by the descendants of those exiles who had found new and happier homes in southern and north-western Europe. At the beginning of the eighteenth century R. David Nieto, the *Haham* of the Spanish and Portuguese Jews in London, was not only a Jewish divine of distinction, acquainted with the niceties of Christian theology, but versatile in the natural sciences, medical and astronomical. He wrote *Maṭṭeh Dan*, his philosophical *magnum opus*, in an elegant Spanish as well as in a clear, fluent Hebrew, and the translation of the Hebrew Prayer Books into Spanish by his son, Isaac Nieto, indicated the fine taste as well as the cultural *pietas* of the Sephardi Jews in London more than two and a half centuries after the Great Expulsion.

Isaac Abravanel was socially, intellectually, and religiously an exemplar of Sephardi Judaism at the end of its tragic eclipse. But though a successful financier, he failed lamentably in this capacity at the close of his Spanish *débâcle*; for, by the strangest of ironies, the material help which he and other wealthy Jews gave to Ferdinand and Isabella for the ultimate conquest of the Moors, brought about the complete unification of Spain not only politically but religiously, and rendered the further presence and the influence of the Jews in that country a practical impossibility. The statesmanship which Abravanel had been able to exercise for the protection of the Jews proved at the crucial moment of no avail; and, like many another Jew who had given invaluable service to his country, he found his devotion to the land he cherished ill requited.

Isaac Abravanel has, therefore, secured his outstanding place in Jewish history not by his worldly success or by his statesmanship but, in a characteristically Jewish way, by his literary labours, notably in the biblical and talmudical fields. In the spare leisure he enjoyed in the earlier part of his life he devoted himself to Jewish studies, his first treatise, entitled '*Aṭereth Zeḳenim* (*The Crown of the Elders*), being composed by him before he reached the age of twenty. In the course of time, he became one of the greatest of Jewish exegetes of the Bible. He wrote commentaries on almost all the books of the Hebrew Scriptures, with the exception of the Hagiographa. In his later years, he deplored the fact that he had not given more of his time to his investigations into the ancient sacred lore of Judaism. The most fruitful literary period of his life was after his exile from Spain, especially when he had left Naples for Messina and thence for Corfu. He settled ultimately at Monopoli, a little town on the Apulian coast, where he found for some time a refuge from political distractions. He arrived at Monopoli at the end of the year 1495 and remained there eight years. In January 1496, he resumed and completed what was to have been his first important work, a commentary on Deuteronomy. The preface to his *Zebaḥ Pesaḥ*, a commentary on the Passover *Haggadah*, which he finished in March 1496, shows him then in a state bordering on despair. For he could not fail to contrast his happy state of yore and the fortunes of his people in Sepharad in former times with those in which he and they now found themselves. But his comments on the first deliverance of his people from bondage not only show him as a ready writer but manifest his unfaltering faith in the future of his people. It is this which gave him, in spite of all, strength to endure. It is this unquenchable confidence in the divine protection that appears in his *Naḥalath 'Aboth* (*The Heritage of the Fathers*) which he wrote as the result of his studies on the *Pirḳé 'Aboth* with his youngest son Samuel. This was, in effect, a literary legacy to his son of twenty-three —who, later, became famous as a Maecenas and champion of his people—leaving him the results of his ripe reflections in a life rich with experience.

In his commentaries, Abravanel shows himself an exegete
who probed deeply and scientifically the literal sense of the
biblical writings, and, unlike Jewish commentators in northern
and eastern Europe, and in spite of the prevailing fanaticism,
he did not hesitate to utilize the expositions of Christian
theologians and availed himself of his acquaintance with the
Greek and Latin classics and Arab literature. He applied
his familiarity with the ways of courts and high politics to the
events of Jewish antiquity, and was thus able to deal with
them from an objectively historical, as distinct from a purely
religious or literary, point of view.

While his philosophical writings were comparatively superficial and remained ephemeral in their influence, they nevertheless helped to keep alive, in circles far beyond the Jewries
of Spanish and Portuguese provenance, those humanistic
aspects of Judaism which became more rare as the concentrated attention to its Halakhic elements narrowed the
intellectual vision of the medieval Jews. He was a thinker—
if not profound, at least guided by a clear mind—who, in an
age of doubt and distress, was able to give to the fundamental
doctrines of Judaism a philosophical basis. Particularly at
Monopoli, where he gathered around him a circle of friends
and disciples, he wrote a commentary, entitled *Shamayim
Hadashim* (*New Heavens*), on the 19th chapter of Moses
Maimonides' *Guide*—a commentary which was destined
to be his last, though uncompleted, literary undertaking.
Other works on Jewish religious philosophy were *Miph'alot
'Elohim* (*The Wondrous Works of God*) on the Creation, and
Rosh 'Amanah (*The Pinnacle of Amanah*: Cant. IV, 8, Amana =
'Emunah, Faith) on the Thirteen Creeds of Moses Maimonides.

His biblical commentaries earned him later on, when a
critical study of the Bible came into vogue, a remarkably wide
recognition among many Christian theologians, and a highly
appreciative Latin biography of Isaac Abravanel by Johann
Heinrich Mai appeared in Germany in 1707.

There is one outstanding feature in his life and writings
which arose out of the tragic events of the time, viz. the
Messianic eschatological hopes which he entertained with a
growing conviction as the gloom gathered around him.

The controversy with Christianity, which he took up with
courage and unfaltering trust in the eventual triumph of
Israel, led him, as it did so many others down to our own
days, to the sure and certain hope of the Restoration of the
Jewish people to its ancient land. In his statesmanlike conception no less than in his faith in the literal fulfilment of the
biblical prophecies, the return of the Jews to Palestine, even
under the suzerainty of the Grand Turk, seemed to him not
only possible but imminent. In his fervent hope he already
saw in his mind's eye the ships carrying the pilgrims to the
Holy Land in order to re-establish there the national foundations of old.

The Jews of those times sorely needed a guide; they cried
out for consolation and for an object in life. Their misery
grew in intensity, and despair took hold of most of them. The
faith and heroism that had sustained them too often gave way
to demoralization. The part assumed by Don Isaac Abravanel
in infusing new strength in those whose hearts had become
faint was thus of outstanding importance. He composed a
trilogy of works under the general title of *Migdol Yeshu'oth*
(*The Tower of Salvation*); these are devoted to an exposition
of Jewish Messianic hopes. It was not only a defence of
Judaism against the ruthless, inexorable pressure of the
dominant and apparently victorious religion of Christendom,
but a positive promise, on the strength of the biblical prophecies, of the imminence of the Redemption, which,
according to his calculations by the system of *Gemaṭria*
based on Daniel xii, he reckoned would take place in the
year 1503.

These three treatises—*Ma'yene hay-Yeshu'ah* (*Wells of Salvation*), *Yeshu'oth Meshiḥo* (*The Salvation of His Anointed*), and
Mashmia' Yeshu'ah (*Proclaiming Salvation*)—were completed in
the years 1496, 1497 and 1498 respectively. They reveal the
state of mind of Abravanel and of his contemporaries and
contain a comprehensive and effective apologia for Judaism.
If, argued Abravanel, all the sufferings predicted by the
prophets have come to the Jewish people, then, of a surety,
they could expect that the consolations similarly promised, as

the result of the faithfulness of Israel to its Covenant with God, would in due time also be fulfilled.

Isaac Abravanel dealt in these works in a masterly way with those age-long hopes which have alone sustained the Jewish people through the agonies which, not only the Sephardi Jews in their martyrdom, but also their kinsfolk and co-religionists in eastern Europe, then and in later times, were likewise to undergo in an equal measure. His writings were, therefore, not only of the time and for the time in which he lived, but were of much more than ephemeral value. The cardinal point of fundamental conflict between Judaism and Christianity—in which they meet as well as from which they differ—was the Messianic hope of the Redemption of Israel and of mankind. In the case of the Jews, the expectations which centred on the arrival of the Anointed promised in the Scriptures were combined with the desire for the fulfilment of the national Restoration of Israel to the Holy Land. The trials which the Jews underwent were interpreted as the חבלי משיח, the "Messianic birth-pangs", the travails which manifested forebodings of his impending coming. Abravanel's messiological writings, and his belief in bodily resurrection, had a considerable effect on future generations, developing, however, cabbalistic views that beclouded the minds of men and led to the pseudo-Messianic movements in the sixteenth and seventeenth centuries.

In reviewing the extraordinarily checkered life of Don Isaac Abravanel, we must come to the conclusion that his true greatness consisted in the fact that he was not only a versatile man of letters, but that what he wrote was imbued with his great personality. In those times, full of bitter humiliation and sorrow for the Jewish people, he, a refugee from Spain, was received with remarkable favour and confidence in circles that could hardly have been otherwise than antipathetic to Jews. In Naples, he was welcomed by Ferdinand I and befriended by his successor, Alfonso; and when this city was conquered by King Charles VIII of France, he joined his royal patron in his flight to Messina. His strength lay obviously not in his material power but in the moral force and loyalty inherent in his personal character.

His personal dignity and the confidence which he inspired among Catholic rulers were most strikingly demonstrated when, on his settlement in Venice in 1503, he was given the honourable task of a diplomatic intervention between the Venetian Republic and King Manuel of Portugal, his native land—King Manuel being a brother of the Duke of Viseu, in whose conspiracy against King John II Abravanel had been disastrously implicated. The international question at issue was one of great consequence and characteristic of the times. The discovery of the sea route to India by the Portuguese Vasco da Gama had brought the virtual monopoly of the trade in spices of the Venetians into jeopardy, and also threatened further conflicts of interests as between the sea-borne trade and that on the overland route to India. This was now amicably settled by a treaty which was concluded through the intervention of Don Isaac Abravanel. The Senate of Venice and the Council of Ten expressed formally on 12 August 1503 their solemn thanks for his services in the following record which has been preserved in the State Archives of Venice:

Quod domino Isaach Abraha(m)[v]anel hebreo qui nuper huc venit ex portugallia. . . .
Che nuy lo habiamo veduto et aldito voluntieri, si per le bone qualità e virtù de la persona sua, si etiam per la materia proposta, et per la bona mente el dimonstra haver, al beneficio et commodo de la Signoria nostra de la qual el sij cum parolle grave et accommodate rengratiato. (The full text is given in the Preface.)

But infinitely more precious than the fleeting recognition of the services which Don Isaac Abravanel rendered to the temporal powers of his day is the gratitude and reverence with which his people recall the Sage of Sepharad who, by his faith in their future, shares in their immortality.

Lecture II

SPAIN IN THE AGE OF ABRAVANEL

BY PROFESSOR I. GONZÁLEZ LLUBERA

SPAIN IN THE AGE OF ABRAVANEL

I

AT the beginning of the fifteenth century the Spanish Peninsula comprised five states. Four were ruled by Christian sovereigns, whilst the fifth was a survival of a defeated and now decadent civilization. It was in the nature of things that this kingdom of Granada should become a province of Christian Castile sooner or later. Wide differences existed between the various Christian states. They differed from one another in their historical origins and language, in their internal organization and laws, economic conditions and artistic aptitudes. They stood for diverging political conceptions. Thus the guiding lines of their policies appeared to be conceptions. Thus the guiding lines of their policies appeared to be unrelated, if not mutually contradictory. Of the Christian states the wealthiest and most prosperous was the united kingdom of Aragon and Catalonia. Under the wise and steady rule of the house of Barcelona it had attained political maturity. It was at the moment the leading power in the Mediterranean. Portugal, under the dynasty of Avis, was planning and was soon to evolve a policy of vast scope, such as would lead to internal prosperity and international importance. Castile remained much poorer in resources than either Portugal or Aragon, notwithstanding the fact that she was in possession of the greater part of Andalusia and the exceedingly fertile plains of Murcia. For a century now she had been rent by civil strife. It seemed as though this state of affairs was to become an endemic feature of her political life.

From her association with the old kingdom of León, Castile had inherited the ideal of Peninsular unity. The rise of the County of Castile to the status of a separate kingdom coincided with the early stages of Cluniac penetration in northern and western Spain. Thus the ideal of Peninsular unity became a local version of the European Crusade. This was an unfortunate development, as a united Spain, a Spain in which the Christian and the Moslem civilizations would have developed side by side under the kings of León and Castile, was a distinct possibility for the territories situated south of the Ebro in the years following upon the disintegration of the Caliphate of Córdoba. The lasting adhesion of Castile to the Crusade spirit prevented this course from being taken.

In the kingdom of Aragon the Crusading ideal had been superseded by other policies of Mediterranean expansion in the course of the thirteenth century, whilst in Portugal it eventually led towards African conquests. In Castile, on the other hand, it had remained unaltered and its survival was to be a constant feature of her future history.

The policy of exclusion that the adoption of the Crusade ideals presupposes was hard to instil into the Spanish people —the Moslems of Al-Andalus were racially more akin to the Spanish Christians than were the latter to the peoples beyond the Pyrenees. By the end of the fourteenth century, however, the feeling of hatred of the infidel had permeated the Christian population of the Spanish kingdoms in general, whilst in Castile it coloured all her plans of political expansion. Castile was thus evolving a policy based on the enforcement of religious conformity within the realm, whilst centralization was to be a basic principle of the internal constitution of the state.

Religious conformity afforded a common basis of collaboration between the Christian states. Constitutional divergences, particularly between Castile and Aragon, had increased ever since the middle of the thirteenth century. The annexation of the territory of Jaén, Córdoba, and Seville, a consequence of the Moslem collapse after Las Navas (1212), led to the creation of vast latifundia—vested in the Military Orders and the nobility—in Estremadura and Ciudad Real. Whilst the conquests of Ferdinand III and Alfonso the Wise afforded some scope to the centralizing tendencies of Castile, the increase of latifundia strengthened the power of the nobility, thus creating a permanent opposition between the Crown and the nobles. Things had taken a different course in Valencia and Majorca after their incorporation in Aragon-

Catalonia under James the Conqueror (1229–38). Both became Catalan in language and institutions; each possessed its own government, councils and parliament. The advanced state of agriculture and the industrial art which prevailed in them under Moslem rule persisted under their new masters. These conditions resulted in the emergence of a prosperous middle class, which, in Valencia as well as in Barcelona, powerfully contributed to establish the supremacy of the Crown. Under a particularly able king (Peter the Ceremonious) the battle against the Aragonese nobles was thus successfully waged once and for all. Then the united kingdoms attained a social stability which offered a sharp contrast to prevailing Castilian conditions.

The subordination of León and Galicia to Castile brought about the rise of the County of Portugal as an independent kingdom (1139). León, which from the outset included Galicia, tended towards the western sea, whilst the trend of Castilian expansion was southwards. Protected on its eastern boundary by a succession of sparsely populated plains, Portugal was able to pursue her own *reconquista* in comparative safety and annex the rich lands along the Atlantic shore, whilst the possession of Lisbon and Oporto marked her for a sea power. But she had to look for allies in case of aggression from the east. In the middle of the fourteenth century the Trastamaras had had to rely on French support in their war against Peter the Cruel. It is not surprising that the foreign policy of Portugal began to gravitate towards England. The first conflict with Castile arose over the succession at the death of King Ferdinand (1385), when the King of Castile claimed the throne. The Portuguese, however, proclaimed João of Avis. Castile invaded Portugal. But the host of the King of Castile was defeated at Aljubarrota. In the following year (1386) the treaty of Windsor between João I and Richard II was signed.

The extinction of the dynasty of Barcelona brought about the election of the Infante Ferdinand of Trastamara to the Aragonese throne (1412). The decision of the representatives at Caspe was the outcome of a movement aiming at the union of Aragon and Castile. The movement was fostered mainly by the Church and the nobility of Aragon proper. Castilian penetration of the kingdom of Aragon was from that time steadily pursued by the Crown. The Catalans often showed their disapproval of the policies inaugurated by the Trastamaras, as it became clear that national interests were being subordinated to dynastic prestige. The attitude of the Catalans to the King during the fifteenth century oscillated between latent opposition and open protest whenever their liberties were threatened. But when the *Generalidad* finally rose against John II it was too late. The war went on for ten years (1462–72), and although in the end national institutions were saved, internal decadence, now accentuated by the economic weakness of Barcelona, was not arrested. Catalonia was at the mercy of the King, and the assimilationist methods pursued by Ferdinand the Catholic could not be effectively countered. In addition, external causes precipitated the rapid decadence of the eastern kingdoms: the rise of a new power in the eastern Mediterranean, Portuguese initiative, and chiefly the exclusion of all but Castilian subjects from the trade with the new Castilian possessions overseas.

In the meanwhile Portugal had become a thalassocracy and was rapidly approaching the zenith of her power. Thirty years after Aljubarrota a nation mainly agricultural had been transformed into a commercial power. It was one of the most striking events in the history of medieval Europe. Portuguese expansion outside the Peninsula started with the conquest of Ceuta by João I (1415). Tangiers was taken in 1471 after earlier unsuccessful attempts. The first siege of that city (1437), when D. Fernando, *o Infante Santo*, was made a prisoner by the Moors should be mentioned.

Of much greater importance were the maritime expeditions carried out under the direction of the Infante D. Henrique and those who after him succeeded in performing the longest feat of navigation hitherto planned by Europeans. Attempts to explore the West African coast, south of Cape Bojador, were made soon after the conquest of Ceuta. Madeira and Porto Santo were occupied in 1418–19, the Azores in 1439. Soon after the death of D. Henrique the Congo was reached, whilst in 1469 Fernão Gomes was establishing the basis of the new empire in the settlement of São Jorge da Mina. When at last the new route to India was opened after the discovery of the Cape and the expedition of Vasco da Gama, the port of Lisbon became the European centre of East Indian trade. In contrast to the Castilian *conquistas* of the sixteenth century, the Portuguese navigations rested upon well-defined plans, scientifically discussed and adequately endowed. They were not the unexpected result of a hazardous adventure. But there was also a widespread national interest in those superb exploits. The explorers could count upon the collaboration— a very intelligent collaboration indeed—of princes and nobles. Thus at the end of the fifteenth century the house of Avis had not only secured national independence, but had also made Portugal a wealthy nation and the centre of a world empire.

Contemporary Castile presented a sorry picture of civil strife and disorder up to the time when Ferdinand and Isabella assumed the government of the realm. Thus it was only in the final third of the century that the Crown was able to attempt the reorganization of the state so as to strengthen the Crown. The power of the nobility was effectively crushed.

Towards the middle of the century that very able statesman, Don Alvaro de Luna, paid with his life (1453) for his attempts in a similar direction. The union of the crowns of Aragon and Castile was now in sight. For the present Ferdinand and Isabella were to be joint sovereigns of Castile, whilst on his father's death Ferdinand would become King of Aragon. On their death both states would be ruled by one king. For a time it seemed as though the Crown of Portugal would fall also to the Heir-Apparent, Prince John. Providence decreed otherwise. At the close of the century Granada was conquered, and in his search for the west route Columbus was to hit on a new continent. In both of those great enterprises, Royal policies were guided by the medieval ideal of the Crusade. In the field of European relations, however, King Ferdinand obeyed more realistic purposes, and his diplomacy was leading to the encirclement of France, thus changing into open rivalry and lasting enmity the traditional friendship between the latter power and the house of Trastamara. Castile had thus assumed the leadership of all the Spains. And at this point our survey stops.

II

The constitution of Christian Spain was incompatible with the existence of religious dissidence in its midst. Jewish institutions were thus tolerated on certain specific conditions and for certain definite purposes. The medieval state aimed at their abolition. Jewish life and culture in Spain were stronger and more diversified than in other parts of medieval Europe. These circumstances permitted Judaism to influence several departments of Spanish life to a greater extent than elsewhere in Christendom, whilst they were able to postpone the issue for a longer period. The final breakdown thus implied not only a process of persecution and enforced assimilation—the Spanish version of a general European policy—but the internal decadence of the Spanish Jewries as well.

Jewish civilization on Spanish soil had moulded itself upon Islamic patterns. Arabic thought and literary forms were adapted to Hebrew. Accordingly poetry, narrative rhymed prose, philosophical and ethical works of a high literary range, flourished in abundance; standard scientific treatises were rendered into Hebrew. All this apart from the superb vitality of rabbinic learning.

Hebrew-Spanish literature is a manifestation of the eleventh and twelfth centuries. It developed in the Moslem succession states and in newly conquered Toledo at a time when Castile had not yet wholly adhered to European conformity. In all its variety it survived the ruin of the Andalusian communities under the rule of the Berber dynasties and flourished still for some time in Toledo, Catalonia and Languedoc. Certain branches of Hebrew literature then reached their highest point of development. One of the greatest names in Rabbinic learning occurs in the community of Girona in Catalonia during the first half of the thirteenth century. But there were also converts to Christianity, as the Disputation of Barcelona

(1263) goes to show. The prestige of Jewish interpreters of Arabic science persisted throughout the century, and along with Hebrew literary *genres* spread from Provence to the south of Italy. The principles of the Lateran Decrees (1179 and 1215) began to make their appearance in Spanish legislation, as may be seen in the *Fuero Real*, the *Leyes del Estilo*, and the *Siete Partidas*. Jewish cultural life in Spain steadily deteriorated in the course of the fourteenth century. Learning in the Jewish communities gave place of precedence to material considerations. Distinguished Jews occupied important posts in the administration. They became physicians and astronomers in the service of the King or prominent members of the nobility. They contributed to the development of vernacular literature, particularly of Spanish, but also of Catalan. Excellent Hebrew was still written in the kingdom of Aragon during the first half of the century, but much less in Castile. Hebrew-Spanish literature, however, had passed its zenith. Material prosperity and influence accrued to the Castilian communities during the times of Alfonso XI and Peter the Cruel (1312–69), whilst popular opposition was fostered mainly by organized ecclesiastical propaganda.

The Castilian civil war between Peter the Cruel and his half-brother Henry of Trastamara (1350–69) marked a turning point at this period of Jewish-Spanish history. During the reign of Henry II a considerable number of *almojarifazgos* were still entrusted to Jews. Previous petitions for restrictive measures, however, were gradually granted: the wearing of the Jewish badge, which up to then had not been enforced, was made compulsory under severe penalties.[1] The exclusion of Jews from office under the Crown and their employment by noblemen were demanded by the representatives at the Cortes of Burgos (1379). These demands were partially granted at first and adopted in their entirety under the administration of John I (1385).[2] A decree of 1380 abolished

[1] Baer (*Die Juden im christlichen Spanien*, Erster Teil. *Urkunden und Regesten*. Vol. I, *Aragonien und Navarra*, Berlin, 1929. Vol. II, *Kastilien, Inquisitionsakten*, Berlin, 1936), II, no. 217.
[2] *Ibid.* no. 220.

Jewish judicial jurisdiction in criminal cases.[1] The measure was prompted by the murder of Joseph Pichon, the Royal *almojarife* at Seville under Henry II. Popular passions were roused to a dangerous pitch by the Canon of Seville and Archdeacon of Écija, Ferran Martínez. He openly advocated from the pulpit not only the destruction of Jewish places of worship, but that of the Seville Jewry as a first step towards the total extinction of Judaism in Christian Spain.

The agitation roused by Ferran Martínez's activities led to the riots of 1391. During the summer of that year Castilian Jewries were looted and a considerable number of Jews were murdered. The infection overspread the kingdom of Aragon: the Jewry of Valencia was wiped out, and the chief Catalan communities were subsequently attacked, beginning with that of Barcelona. Drastic measures were taken by the Royal administration, both in Aragon and Castile, so as to put a stop to the wave of destruction with the consequent loss in Royal revenue.[2]

In connection with the propagation of the Castilian anti-Jewish movement in Aragon, it should be noted that the repressive measures, which were enacted in Castile during the latter part of the fourteenth century, had no counterpart in the former kingdom up to the beginning of the fifteenth. The general tendencies, however, were there all the same, and were reflected in the restriction of Jewish participation in the administration of the Royal treasury in the course of

---

[1] Baer, II, no. 227.

[2] See Baer, II, p. 233. On the attitude of the authorities towards Ferran Martínez, see Amador, *Historia social, política y religiosa de los judíos en España y Portugal*, Madrid, 1875–6, II, pp. 338 ff. and the documents included in Baer's repertory (II, nos. 221, 247, 259). The following quotation from a Royal appeal to the city of Burgos is illuminating: "Yo el Rey...Sepades que se ha sabido como agora en estos dias passados en las muy nobles cibdades de Sevilla e Cordova, por enduzimientos...que fizo...el arçediano de Ecija, que algunos de las gentes menudas de las dichas cibdades, como omes rosticos e de poco entendimiento, non parando mientes al yerro...e non temiendo a Dios nin a mi jostiçia...que fueron contra los judios que estaban en las aljamas de las dichas cibdades e mataron pieça dellos e a otros robaron, e a otros robaron, e a otros por fuerça fizieron que se tornassen christianos; por lo qual los judios que estaban en las aljamas...han sido espoblados. De lo qual yo ove muy grand enojo, por que viene a mi dello muy grand deserviçio" Segovia, 16 June 1391 (Baer, II, no. 248).

the fourteenth century. It is also worth stressing the fact that stern measures were taken to prevent the extension of disorder[1] and the ringleaders were executed in Barcelona.

Wholesale desertion of the ancestral faith was the most significant effect of the riots. "For the first and only time in human memory, the Jewish morale broke down", says a modern authority. Those Jewries against which the terror was most savage were more deeply affected: Seville and Córdoba, Talavera and Maqueda, Orihuela, Lorca and Murcia. But extraordinary scenes of mass conversion were witnessed in Valencia and Catalonia. The conversion of Rabbi Solomon hal-Levi, his five sons and other members of his family, was a sign of the times. It took place in Burgos a year before the disorders. The subsequent career of the Santa Marias in Church and State is typical of the new social class of the *conversos* in fifteenth-century Spain.

Conversionist activities were one of the chief purposes of the order of the Friars Preacher. A prominent member of the Order at the time was Vincent Ferrer. He devoted a good deal of his energies to advance the cause of proselytism among the Jews. His truly remarkable personality, the vehemence of his convictions, the power of his appeal, his tireless energy, were bound to succeed against a cowed and persecuted minority. Possibly he had been the determining agent in the conversion of the Santa Marias, and it is no exaggeration to say that through him the flower of Rabbinic scholars in Aragon went over to Christianity. There were of course some notable exceptions (Ḥaśdai Crescas, Joseph Albo, and others). Prevailing opinions about Messianism were partly responsible for several of these conversions.

It was under Dominican auspices that the example of Paris (1240) was followed on several occasions in the kingdom of Aragon. It consisted in staging a theological disputation between learned Rabbis and Christian scholars. Partly at

---

[1] *Ibid.* I, no. 446, 4. It is a letter from King John I of Aragon to his *merino* at Saragossa. Referring to the possibility of Ferran Martínez coming to Aragon, the King writes as follows: "E queremos que si el arçidiano de Castiella...viene en aquexas partes e continua las locuras que se dizen dell...aquell arçidiano nos sea embiado luego o por tierra o por agua" Barcelona, 4 May 1391.

the instigation of a convert this procedure was repeated now under the auspices of Benedict XIII in the town of Sant Mateu, not far from Penyíscola, where the Pope resided. The sessions, which lasted for more than a year, were opened by the Pope in February, 1413. By these means it was hoped to bring about the conversion of the remaining Jewries of Aragon. One result of this protracted conference interests us particularly; the issue of the Bull of Benedict XIII concerning the Jews (1415). This document, however, was preceded in Castile by the Ordinances, sometimes mentioned after the name of the Regent, Queen Catherine (Valladolid, 1412).[1] They had been drawn up under the advice of Santa Maria the Elder, who had been promoted to the See of Burgos, and in his capacity of Chancellor of the realm was also a member of the Council of Regency during the King's minority. The regulations were intended for all infidels, whether Jews or Moors, subjects of the King of Castile. They aimed at the total segregation of the Jews from the Christian population. The Jews were forbidden to engage in most trades and professions. They were strictly confined to their own quarters. Their freedom of movement within the realm and the right to emigrate were curtailed. It was rendered illegal for a Jew to try to prevent a member of his own family from adopting the Christian faith. All these prohibitions were also embodied in the Papal Bull. The latter, however, included further restrictions: it was made illegal for a Jew to possess a Talmud or any other book connected with Talmudic doctrine, or a Hebrew book containing anti-Christian statements. A Jewish community was allowed only one synagogue and all Jews above twelve years of age were to attend conversionist exhortations three times a year on stated Sundays. Pope Benedict's Bull became the law of the land for the kingdom of Aragon, by virtue of an ordinance of Ferdinand I of Trastamara (Valencia, 23 July 1415).[2]

The policy of indiscriminate conversion, however, defeated its own ends, whilst the disappearance of the Jewish *aljamas*

---

[1] Baer, II, no. 275.
[2] *Ibid.* I, no. 513.

did not commend itself to the Royal administrations. Consequently all measures tending to regularize and stabilize the position of the communities were supported by the Crown.[1]

The period of *converso* ascendancy extended to the later decades of the fifteenth century. The ascendancy, however, did not remain undisturbed in Castile for much longer than one generation. During the first half of the century, the converted Jew, now in full possession of civil rights, made his presence felt in every department of life, in Church and State, in commerce and letters. In Aragon the peak of the wave was reached somewhat later. In Castile popular reaction voiced its opposition against the *conversos* for the first time towards the middle of the century. From that time, up to the years following upon the establishment of the New Inquisition, the conditions under which Jewish communities were allowed to exist remained fairly stable. The most cruel provisions in the above-mentioned enactments were adopted at the instigation of notorious *conversos*, but they were never rigidly enforced. In Castile a very conspicuous difference in the treatment of the Jews continued to exist between the cities, in which Jewish legislation was, as a rule, strictly applied, and in the country domains of the nobility and the Royal household, in which things went on very much as before the restrictions were imposed. This state of affairs explains the presence of Jewish physicians in the Court of John II and Henry IV, that the Chief Rabbi Abraham Benveniste was counted amongst the trusted advisers of the former in the early years of his reign, that Jews were still appointed to farm the taxes, and, more significant still, that a Rabbi would undertake a vernacular version of the Bible at the request of a Grand Master of Calatrava (1422–30).

It is not surprising that Don Pablo de Santa Maria persisted in his virulent attacks almost to his deathbed (his *Scrutinium* was written in 1434),[2] and that his son and suc-

---

[1] An important document showing the effort to protect Jewish life under particularly adverse conditions is the measure of reorganization of the Castilian communities issued by the Rabbinical synod held at Valladolid (1432). It is included in Baer's repertory (II, no. 287).

[2] Amador, III, pp. 38 *seqq*.

cessor in the See of Burgos pleaded for the enforcement of Benedict XIII's Bull at the General Council of Basle (1442). The Papal Bull to that effect was published in Toledo without the Royal assent. This action the Royal administration answered with the enactment of Arévalo (1443). The measure obviously aimed at effecting some relief in the position of the Jews.[1] It was, however, merely an episode in the long feud between Don Alvaro de Luna and his enemies, with whom the Santa Marias were in league. The tragic end of Don Alvaro (1453) was mainly due to the enmity of the *conversos*. It also marked the beginning of their decadence in Castile. The first episode in the movement against them had been enacted four years before in Toledo.[2]

The *pragmática* of Arévalo has a counterpart in the measures taken in Aragon under the regency of Queen Maria (1437). The reason for this departure from the enactment of Ferdinand I was the plight of the Jewish communities and the pressing needs of the Treasury, at a time when the ambitious plans of Alfonso the Magnanimous in Italy and the defeat of the Aragonese in the naval battle of Ponza (1435) had taxed to the utmost the resources of the kingdom. The revenue from Jewish sources did not increase. The wealthy Jewries of Barcelona, Valencia, and Majorca had disappeared, whilst the *conversos* had increased in considerable numbers. There was a notable difference, however, in the social aspect of the problem between the Catalan-speaking countries and Aragon proper. In the former the *conversos* remained a separate class. They engaged, as a rule, in commercial pursuits. Catalan literature—in spite of their large influence in Castilian letters —was not enriched by their contributions. In Aragon, on the other hand, marriages between Christians and *conversos* were encouraged. Their proportion in the professions was large, possibly larger than in Castile. Their political influence was considerable, particularly in the reign of John II. The negotiations leading to the marriage of Ferdinand, Prince of

---

[1] Amador, III, pp. 583 *seqq.*

[2] See H. Pflaum, in *Rev. ét. juives*, vol. LXXXVI (1928), pp. 131 *seqq.*; Baer, II, no. 302.

Sicily, and Isabella, a daughter of John II of Castile, were successfully concluded, thanks to the diplomacy of Mossen Pedro de la Caballería the Younger. Thus the main ambition of the King of Aragon—as it paved the way towards the conquest of the Castilian crown—was realized.

The Jewish communities of Portugal had lived at peace with their Christian neighbours throughout the fourteenth century. They had loyally helped the house of Avis in the national emergency of 1385. The Royal treasury remained in Jewish hands in the reign of João I. The kingdom had opened its gates to Jewish refugees from Castile in 1391. This generous attitude of the Crown gave rise to popular opposition, which increased rapidly when it became known that a large proportion of the immigrants had been baptized and their purpose in coming was to renounce Christianity. The Crown was then compelled to adopt restrictive measures. A decree of 1400 ordered the separation of the Jewish from the Christian population. Other measures included regulations aiming at the destruction of Jewish estates. The position of the Jewish communities was made more precarious by the adoption of the Bull of Benedict XIII in the reign of D. Duarte (1433–8). In Portugal, however, to a greater measure than in contemporary Castile, the provisions of the law were not uniformly enforced. The public career of the Abravanels provides an example of this attitude towards the Jews in the higher councils of the kingdom.

III

Isaac Abravanel was born in Lisbon in the last year of King Duarte's reign. His father, Don Judah, held office in the household of King João I's youngest son, the Infante D. Fernando, who remained a prisoner of the Moors in Fez from the year of Isaac's birth till 1448. Isaac's grandfather was an *almojarife* of the city of Seville in the days of Henry II of Castile. He had been compelled to adopt Christianity in 1391. He left Castile and returned to the faith of his fathers as soon as he settled in Portugal. Financial skill, for which

Isaac became well known, was a tradition of the family. Don Judah, our writer's great-grandfather, was *almojarife* under Ferdinand IV of Castile,[1] whilst we hear of Juce Abrabanell in the household of Henry II during the civil war (1367).[2]

Isaac's biography in Portugal coincides with the reign of Afonso V. The reign opened with a turbulent minority, followed by a war waged by the young King against his uncle D. Pedro, the former Regent, who met his death in the field at Alfarrobeira (1449). The following decades saw explorations carried out under Henry the Navigator and his collaborators, and several campaigns in Morocco. In the latter, Jewish finance played an important part. The expedition, which ended in the surrender of Arzila and Tangiers, was successful, thanks to the able administration of the King's treasury, for which Isaac Abravanel was responsible at the time. The Jewish contribution to the maritime undertakings, both in the scientific and the financial aspect, was considerable. It would be mistaken, however, to think that a reversal of policy had taken place in the official attitude towards the Jews. In all essential points Portugal differed but little in this respect from the other Spanish kingdoms. Here, as elsewhere, a distinction must be drawn between the nobility and the middle classes. Historical judgments [regarding Portuguese policy towards the Jews during the period in question] ought not to be based on evidence of an incidental nature, such as cases of personal consideration or friendship between individual noblemen and certain Jews of outstanding ability. The protests by ecclesiastics and by the towns against the increase of Jewish participation in the administration of Royal revenues were symptomatic. The position is perhaps better illustrated by the sequel to the Lisbon riot of 1449, when an attack against the Jewry took place. The ringleaders were condemned to death, but the executions had to be abandoned in view of the dangerous turn of popular opposition, which now seemed to be directed against the King. It is

[1] Benavides, *Memorias de D. Fernando IV de Castilla*, Madrid, 1860, II, p. 760.
[2] Baer, I, no. 277.

not surprising that Jewish legislation remained, during the rest of the century, that contained in the *Ordenações Afonsinas*. This compilation had been in progress during the reigns of João I and D. Duarte. It had been published in the first year of Afonso V. The *Ordenações* confirmed earlier legislation with regard to the status of Jews and Moors. Jews were excluded from public office, whilst protection was afforded to the *conversos*.[1]

João II, who succeeded his father in 1481, was intent on strengthening the authority of the Crown in the early years of his reign. His conduct in the furtherance of his aims was typical of the times. At the beginning he had to confront the enmity of his uncle D. Fernando, Duke of Braganza, who had been plotting against him. D. Fernando was in secret correspondence with the King and Queen of Castile, and was encouraging Ferdinand to invade Portugal. D. João II had proof of conspiracy since 1481, but did not proceed against the plotters till May, 1483, when the Duke and his brother were both condemned to death. The young Duke of Vizeu, although involved in the plot, was spared for a time. How far Isaac and Joseph Abravanel were implicated we do not know. Their connection with the Duke and his family was matter of common knowledge. Soon after the execution of D. Fernando, both Isaac and Joseph fled the country. Their property was confiscated after the death of the Duke of Vizeu (August, 1484). A year before he left Portugal, Isaac's house had been looted by the mob in an anti-Jewish riot.

The policy of João II towards the Jews was not more prejudiced than that of his predecessors. At a time when the immigration of Castilian 'anusim (forced converts) was assuming large proportions, the administration took a middle course. It did not favour the extremists. Thus when the cities of Lisbon and Oporto decided upon the expulsion of the Jews from their midst (March–April 1487), the measure was declared illegal.

Isaac Abravanel settled in Toledo. The earliest evidence of his presence in Castile in Spanish documents, however, is

[1] Amador, III, pp. 183–5.

rather late (February, 1488). At the time he was domiciled at Alcalá de Henares.[1] Joseph became a tax collector in the lands of the Grand Master of Calatrava.[2] Since his arrival in Castile, Isaac was in touch with the *Rab de la Corte*, Abraham Senior. Those were years when the war against Granada absorbed all the resources of the state, whilst the main preoccupation in the domain of home affairs was the problem of the *conversos*, which had taken a grave turn since the times of Henry IV (1454–74).

Opposition to the *conversos* was based on religious grounds. But it was perhaps to the same extent based on economic and social conditions. It appeared most vividly at a time when popular hatred against the nobility was also prevalent. It was clear that under the regime inaugurated by Ferdinand and Isabella a solution of the problem would soon be attempted. Thus in the repression of *converso* influence several currents concurred, and it was incumbent upon the Crown to control the public reaction whilst increasing its authority and prestige. In 1459 the Franciscan Alonso de Espina, who was of *converso* origin, published an anti-Jewish work entitled *Fortalitium Fidei*. The originality of this work lies in its attack on the *'anusim*, and in a strong plea for the institution of inquisitorial procedure as a remedy against false professions of Christianity. The agitation against the *conversos* soon led to frequent riots, particularly since the attacked began to take measures of defence. The problem indeed played an important part in the civil disorders of 1465–74. The diversion of public passions meant a respite for the Jewish communities, as shown by the decisions of the Cortes (1462). But a few years later (1469) they were still clamouring for the exclusion of Jews from the *almojarifazgos*,[3] whilst in 1471 the Jewish quarter at Segovia was looted.

A short time after the almost clandestine wedding of Isabella and Ferdinand, the partisans of the princess carried out an attack against the *conversos* of Valladolid (1470). It was hoped in such a way to assuage public displeasure: the close associations between the Trastamaras and the Aragonese

---

[1] Baer, II, no. 362, note.   [2] *Ibid.*   [3] *Ib.* no. 322.

conversos were notorious, as it was also known that Isabella professed open gratitude to Abraham Senior for his loyalty to her as shown more than once in difficult times.[1] Incidental diversions were not likely to deceive the leaders of the anti-*conversos* movement. Their goal was the persecution of heresy carried out in a systematic manner by the Church with the assent of the Crown. The Queen had to act, particularly when the Pope granted power to the Bishop of Trevisa, Nicholaus Franco, for an inquisition to be carried out in all ecclesiastical institutions in Castile (1 August 1475).[2] The Crown then entrusted the Archbishop of Seville, Don Pedro González de Mendoza, a notorious friend of the *conversos*, with the commission of investigation into the charges of heresy preferred against prominent *conversos* by the Prior of the Franciscans, Fray Alonso de Ojeda, and several clergymen of Seville. The Archbishop inaugurated a policy of conciliation, to the discomfiture of the extremists. During the stay of the Queen in Córdoba (1478) Fray Alonso pleaded to her for the application of more drastic measures, whilst he urged further charges against the *conversos*. By the end of that year powers had been granted by the Pope to the Castilian sovereigns for the appointment of Inquisitors. The first appointments were made in the following year. Further powers were asked from the Pope regarding the imposition of the extreme penalty. These were also granted. The Sevillian *conversos* proceeded to defend themselves. A rising was plotted, but it was discovered in time, and the ringleaders, all influential citizens, were executed in the first *auto-de-fé*, which was held in Seville on 6 February 1481.

Two years after, the New Inquisition became one of the Councils of State, and its jurisdiction was extended to the kingdom of Aragon. The *conversos* of Saragossa protested against the novel institution, and the inquisitor Pedro de Arbués was murdered by a prominent member of that class. Barcelona strongly objected to the introduction of a further instrument of Royal domination, and the Castilian Inquisitors were ordered to leave the city (1485). It took three years of

[1] Amador, III, p. 280.   [2] Baer, II, no. 327.

negotiation and threats from the King before the institution began its labours in Catalonia.

The Holy Office, as the new institution came to be known, became an organ in the machinery of the state, one of the political departments of the new realm. Religious conformity was indispensable to the unity of the state and the New Inquisition was established to further that aim. Indirectly, the suppression of infidelity within the realm was a postulate in that order of things. The repercussions of Inquisitorial activities on the life of the Jewish communities were soon felt. An Inquisitorial decision compelled the Jews to leave Andalusia (1483).[1] A reawakening of anti-Jewish feeling, apart from the persecution of the *conversos*, was noticeable throughout the realm. The Cortes had urged the enforcement of existing regulations regarding the intercourse between Jews and Christians, particularly *conversos* (1480).[2] A measure of expulsion of the Jews was in the minds of responsible people. It was withheld only owing to the war against Granada (1481–92). Without Jewish co-operation it would have been impossible for Castile to carry on the struggle to its successful conclusion. Jewish help was of decisive importance both in the financial aspect and in the organization of army supplies in the conquest of Malaga (1487), the siege of Baza (1489), and Granada (1491). The close co-operation of Abraham Senior and Isaac Abravanel eased the stringent financial situation of the treasury. Under their able administration solvency was restored, even prosperity, in the midst of the most costly war Castile had undertaken so far. Had human gratitude ruled political decisions, the conquest of Granada would have meant a measure of freedom for the Jews. As it was, the slightest pretext was bound to lead to the inevitable issue. The problem of the *'anuŝim* was not easily solved. The rigid application of the law did not prevent contact between *conversos* and adherents to the ancestral faith. Popular agitation did not abate. On the contrary, it was growing more violent. And the Holy Office exploited the situation to the full. A story of ritual murder (1490–1) sufficed to bring

[1] Baer, II, nos. 337, 344.   [2] Amador, III, p. 286; Baer, II, no. 335.

matters to a head. Three months after the fall of Granada the edict of expulsion was published. By the end of July of that memorable year all Jews in the dominions of Ferdinand and Isabella were forced either to accept Christianity or else to leave the country. Thus Isaac Abravanel and his family left Spain for Italy. Abraham Senior and his family became *conversos*. They adopted Christianity on 15 June 1492, at Valladolid, the King and Queen acting as their godparents.

The initial stages in the process of Spanish unity were thus accompanied by measures of injustice and the denial of human rights. In the progress towards power and dominion to which the Catholic sovereigns were leading their peoples, the Exodus of 1492 was an augury of decadence.

It is indeed symbolic that the first transatlantic navigation, an undertaking financed very largely with Jewish money and accomplished by a man perhaps of *converso* descent, coincided with the expulsion of the Jews and their exile from Spain. The man whose memory we honour stands out as a symbol of the noble tradition of Jewish-Spanish learning, ability and devotion to the throne. He was a man who, in an age of intellectual decadence and moral defeatism, revived the glories of the Spanish school of biblical exegesis. More important still, he was an example of fortitude and steadfastness. If we seek the reason for Abravanel's greatness, we can find the answer in his character: Abravanel was a truly religious man, and his learning and his life were built upon the Rock and the Redeemer.

Lecture III

ABRAVANEL'S LITERARY WORK

BY DR M. GASTER

ABRAVANEL'S LITERARY WORK

THE object of the present study is to describe and discuss the literary work of Isaac Abravanel. In order, however, that this may be seen and appreciated in true perspective, against the setting of its time and the influence which moulded it, it will be advisable to commence with a brief account of the philosopher's life.

Don Isaac Abravanel, the last representative of the golden period in the life of the Jews in Spain, was born in Lisbon in 1437 and died in Venice in 1508. According to an assertion made by himself on several occasions, he was a lineal descendant of the house of David—a nobility of pedigree with which the whole tenor of his life and character was in closest accord. His father, Judah Abravanel, held a Court position as treasurer to Alphonso V of Portugal, whilst his grandfather, Samuel—a wealthy refugee from the persecutions prevailing in Castile—had long established himself in Portugal as a Maecenas of Jewish letters and a leading personality in the communal life of his brethren. By virtue of his position, Samuel enjoyed free *entrée* to the Court, and mingled with the most distinguished society in the capital. Such influence and affluence ensured for the young Isaac an education in the best contemporary style, embracing, on the one hand, the meticulous study of the Bible and of Hebrew literature, and, on the other, a sound schooling in such "secular" subjects as ancient and modern languages and philosophy. The combination of Jewish and non-Jewish lore which this education evinced, was later to serve its recipient in good stead, for it enabled him to place his work upon the basis of a larger European humanism, rather than upon that of a narrower Rabbinic dialectic. Moreover, it enlarged the range of authority upon which the young scholar might draw, and also furnished him with the necessary equipment for meeting specious arguments of those Christian theologians who endeavoured in public disputations to convince one or other Jewish Rabbi of the Messianic claims of Jesus on the strength of the Bible and Talmud itself. To meet such attacks, a knowledge of the vernacular and of Latin were absolutely indispensable, so that the twofold character of Isaac's education served also a practical end. But Isaac was not to remain within the four walls of his study. Alfonso V, quick to recognize his great financial ability, appointed him one of his chief treasurers. Under the young man's administration, the King's income grew steadily, whilst its treasurer was able to cultivate the friendship of the nobles of the land, among his most intimate friends being the Duke of Braganza and his family. Abravanel used his wealth not only to support scholars and the poor among his people, but also to provide ransom for Jews sold into captivity after the capture of Avilla. Through his great influence, he averted the execution of evil decrees and the consequent persecution which threatened the Jews of Portugal.

With the death of Alfonso, the wheel turned. His son John II, a tyrant and self-seeker, anxious to enrich himself and to eliminate the influence of the nobles, invented a plot alleged to have been hatched by the Duke of Braganza, whom, in consequence, he beheaded and whose vast properties he confiscated. Abravanel would also have been implicated in this alleged plot had not a friend warned him of the impending danger. Thereupon, collecting what he could, he fled in an almost miraculous manner with his family to Spain, making for Toledo. It was a terrible blow, but he sought and found consolation in his beloved books. He reproached himself with having neglected his studies and saw in his troubles the punishment for that neglect. Thus he started to write his Commentary to the historical books of the Bible. With such energy and enthusiasm did he labour, that he finished the commentary on Joshua in fourteen days and within three months the whole manuscript was completed. Long before that he had already composed the commentary to the Pentateuch. But of this more later.

Abravanel's reputation as a great financier had gone before him, with the result that when Ferdinand found his land impoverished after the war with the Moors, he at once sought him out. Abravanel was summoned to the Court and appointed chief treasurer. Once again the finances of the country prospered. Abravanel became a favourite at Court where he also made friends with a large number of the nobility and, among them, with several scholars.

Soon, however, the clouds began to gather. The sinister Dominicans, with Torquemada at their head, were able at last to prevail upon Ferdinand and Isabella. Styling themselves the "Catholic Monarchs" and regardless of the benefits which they had derived from the Jews, and quite unconscious of the deadly blow which they would thus inflict alike upon the arts and sciences, the commerce and industry of Spain, they resolved to expel them. These, although they had, in fact, lived in the Iberian Peninsula for close upon 1500 years, had now to take staff into hand and embark upon their long wandering over the face of the globe in search of lands willing to receive them. First and foremost among them as their guide and luminary, Abrạvanel had proceeded to the Court of King Ferdinand I of Naples and induced him to offer an asylum to the persecuted Jews. Others went to different parts of Italy, some to Navarre, some to Holland, and, not long afterwards, the doors of the Turkish Empire were opened widely by the Sultan Bayezid, who offered unlimited hospitality, freedom from taxation, liberty to develop a communal life, and, above all, freedom in matters of religion.

But fate seemed to pursue Abravanel. For a short while he was able to live in peace at Naples, but not long afterwards Naples was captured by Charles and later became a Spanish province. The governor, Don Pedres, did his best and tried to be friendly to the Jews. But this conciliatory attitude was overruled, and a reign of typical terror ensued. A number of the Jews fled to Turkey and others followed their brethren to different parts of Italy. Among the latter were, in all probability, the three sons of Abravanel, Judah, Joseph, and Samuel. The Duke of Este received the immigrants with liberality, and they settled in large numbers, especially in Ferrara.

Abravanel, however, shared the fate of the unfortunate King Ferdinand and withdrew with him to Sicily, repairing after the death of Ferdinand to Corfu. Subsequently he settled in Monopoli, near Apulia, by Naples. Here, in his retreat, impoverished and heartbroken, he concentrated his literary activity on composing works which might bring comfort and consolation to his stricken brethren, and then removed to Venice.

Appointed financial secretary to the Doge and Signoria, Abravanel used his position to bring about an understanding between the native government of Venice and that of the Portuguese, bringing to the task single-minded disregard of the hardships and trials which the latter had previously inflicted upon him personally. In 1508, the great teacher passed away in his 72nd year, and was buried at Padua. Of his three sons, two—Judah and Joseph—qualified as physicians, whilst the third—Samuel—succeeded his father as financial secretary to the Doge. He married his niece Benvenida, became very wealthy and his house was the recognized centre for the *intelligentsia* and nobility. The Doge even entrusted the education of his daughter to Benvenida.

But all this glory was not to last for long. The family of Abravanel scattered farther. One of them, a contemporary of Menasseh ben Israel, surnamed Dormido, was among the first of those who signed a petition to Cromwell and became the first President of the London community of Bevis Marks.

So much by way of general introduction. We may now turn to the literary activity of Abravanel. As already remarked, Don Isaac Abravanel was the last representative of the glorious tradition of the Jews in Spain. He combined deep religious faith with a gift for philosophic speculation, and his style is not only lucid, but a veritable masterpiece of Hebrew prose. Indeed, the introductions to many of his works, written in rhymed prose, read almost like the *Maḳamat* of *Ḥariẓi* or the best work of Immanuel of Rome. He is able to twist and adapt biblical expressions with uncanny felicity, and his happiness in this respect evidences a rare combination

PLATE I

Eleanor of Toledo

Painted by Bronzino, National Museum, Berlin.

Eleanora, Duchess of Florence, was educated by Benvenida, daughter of Jacob
Abravanel, niece and daughter-in-law of Don Isaac Abravanel.

of biblical knowledge and linguistic creativity. Yet for all this precious dexterity, his style is simple, even if the theme be an abstruse point of metaphysics. His interpretation of the text, whilst being generally rational, verges on the allegorical and symbolic, especially in passages dealing with the eschatological problems of the Messianic age. The very titles of his books evince his mastery of the Hebrew language, consisting always of two words, cunningly wrested from one or other scriptural context.

The literary activity of Abravanel can be considered under three heads, viz. (1) biblical commentaries, (2) philosophic writings, and (3) works treating of the Messianic age. It is this last group which is for us the most significant.

Biblical Commentaries

Abravanel's commentaries on the several books of the Bible will form the subject of a separate contribution to this symposium. It is therefore unnecessary to dilate upon them here, and a few general observations will serve our present purpose adequately. Abravanel's commentaries reveal, in striking fashion, a characteristic which permeates all his work, namely, the power of appreciating the inner and deeper significance of the Sacred Text without recourse to mystical interpretations. His commentaries, it may be said, combine the gifts of inner divination with those of more outward exegesis. Moreover, Abravanel is careful not to ignore the examination of those wider issues which, though not arising directly from the interpretation of any one or other verse, constitute nevertheless the indispensable background for the comprehensive understanding of the whole. Thus, he discusses in some detail the ancient system of social government in Israel, and likewise its methods of trade and commerce. Nor is it only in point of *content* that his originality shows itself. This also extends to the *form* of his commentaries. Imitating, in all probability, the model of his Christian contemporaries, Abravanel is the first Jewish scholar to introduce the system of prefacing each commentary with a general introduction to the book with which it deals. These introductions, however, whilst witnessing to the ordered plan of his work, betray, at the same time, one of Abravanel's most pronounced weaknesses; they are inordinately prolix and long-winded, substituting repetition and involution for that brevity which is the soul of wit and which should be the virtue of exegetes. Nevertheless, despite this defect of style, Abravanel takes his place in biblical scholarship as the last of the great Jewish commentators. Unfortunately, he did not live to see more than three of his works in print. These were published at Constantinople in the years 1505 and 1506. The *locale* of their publication is surprising, since it would appear that round about this time (i.e. 1488–92, and possibly later) Naples itself was a prominent centre of Hebrew printing and probably also of literary activity. Thus, within this period, the presses of Naples produced no less important works than an edition of the Bible, the celebrated Canon of Avicenna, Baḥya's Commentary to the Pentateuch, ibn Ezra's commentary, and other books of considerable significance. It may well be that the subsequent occupation of the city in 1495 by Charles VIII of France, or its later domination by the Spanish, following Gonzalo of Cordova's victory at Garigiliano in 1502, drove away the native Hebrew printers, as happened likewise in other places.

The brothers Nahamias, who printed the volumes in question at Constantinople, would appear to have been refugees from Spain or Portugal, a view supported, perhaps, by the significant fact that several Hebrew *incunabula*, printed shortly before, indeed emanated from the presses of Ixar,[1] Leiria, and Lisbon. The Jewish printers of such cities as these evidently fled as refugees and settled in Salonica and Constantinople, whither they brought their original type, and when the Jews were, in turn, driven out of Naples through the advent of the French and Spanish armies, they must have taken the manuscripts of Abravanel with them and so helped to have them printed at Salonica or Constantinople. The other works of Abravanel were printed long after

[1] E.g. Jacob Ben Asher's *'Oraḥ Ḥayyim* (1485).

his death, two of them, viz. his commentary on Maimonides' *Guide of the Perplexed* and his *Yeshu'oth Meshiḥô*, only in the nineteenth century, after a lapse of some three hundred years.

Philosophic Writings

It falls outside the scope of the present paper to discuss in detail the philosophical ideas of Abravanel. This is reserved for another contribution to our symposium. My own allotted province is confined rather to what may be described as the Messianic speculations of the great teacher. Nevertheless, there is just one of his purely philosophic writings which may claim a word in this place, since its title is somewhat misleading. I refer to the treatise entitled *Shamayim Ḥadashim* (*New Heavens*) (cf. Is. LXVI, 22).

At the first blush it might appear as if this were an eschatological work, dealing with the Messianic era. Such, however, is not the case. The title refers rather to the creation of the world, and the subject is a discussion of the time-honoured philosophic problem whether the world was created by God *ex nihilo* or whether He formed it out of pre-existent matter. Following Maimonides, Abravanel holds that the world had no existence prior to its creation by God. He adheres entirely to the theories prevalent at the time, which he had also accepted from his predecessors, concerning the existence of spheres and the intellects governing them. Astrology was for Abravanel an undisputed science revealing the truth. Moreover, being a sound mathematician, he was able to utilize an impressive amount of mathematical knowledge in support of those intricate calculations and historical combinations of which he availed himself, not only in interpreting the Sacred Text, but also in determining, according to his lights, the history of the world in general, and of the Jews in particular.

Miph'aloth 'Elohim

The same method of reasoning is also to be found in his work *Miph'aloth 'Elohim*, the title of which derives from Ps. LXVI, 5 and may be rendered *The Works of God*. A full discussion of these and similar philosophical treatises falls outside my present sphere, but it may be remarked, by way of general comment, that Abravanel consistently shows himself acquainted with all the leading theories of his predecessors, Gentile as well as Jewish. Moreover, like Maimonides, he refuses to regard philosophy as a purely academic science, but subjects it ever to the service of religion and uses it in order to prove rationally that which is apprehended by the supra-rational and supersensuous instrument of Faith.

Rosh 'Amanah

This last-named tendency appears especially in his work *Rosh 'Amanah*. By clever verbal dexterity, Abravanel here takes two words from Song of Songs IV, 8, where they mean simply "the top of Mount Amanus", to denote "The Essential of Faith" (i.e. *'amanah* = *'emunah*). The object of this work is to examine, from a religio-philosophical point of view, the value of the Thirteen Principles of Faith formulated by Maimonides in his commentary on the *Mishnah* (*Sanhedrin* IX, *Ḥéleḳ*). Abravanel pursues his usual method, first framing a series of questions—"doubts", as he calls them— arranged *seriatim* in the order of the "Thirteen Principles", and then proceeding to answer them in the light of his own conclusions. In the course of these answers, he engages in polemic not only against Ḥasdai Crescas, but also, and more particularly, against Joseph Albo, author of the celebrated *Sepher 'Iḳḳarim*. Abravanel attaches especial importance to the contention that the term *'Iḳḳar* must be interpreted, in a wide sense, to denote a fundamental tenet of religious faith, and he rejects the view that it is equivalent merely to a cardinal injunction of the Law. Inveighing vehemently against a purely nomistic view, he argues that the *'iḳḳarim* of Judaism necessarily includes such cardinal elements of the Jewish religious complex as belief in the Resurrection of the Dead, the Last Judgement and the Advent of the Messiah, although none of these things is mentioned explicitly in the Law, but deduced only from the Prophets and Sacred Writings.

Rosh 'Amanah was first printed at Constantinople, probably in 1506. The identity of the printers is not altogether certain, but it is probably the same as those responsible for the two previous works. The type is the same, though there are slight differences in the watermarks.

Curiously enough, this significant treatise was practically ignored by the Jewish public, whereas it was the subject of considerable discussion, and even of would-be refutation, at the hands of Christian theologians. The Jews, it would appear, were less interested in questions of dogma than were the Gentiles. But of this more hereafter.

'Aṭereth Zeḳenim

Another of Abravanel's philosophic writings which claims attention is his *'Aṭereth Zeḳenim (The Crown of the Aged)* (cf. Prov. xvii, 6). This is an exposition of the passage in Exod. xxiii, beginning, "Behold, I will send mine angel before thee". Abravanel expresses surprise at the fact that previous commentators have not paid adequate attention to this remarkable incident in the career of Moses, conditioning, as it does, much of the Lawgiver's activity and determining, to a large degree, his position. Abravanel introduces his discussion with a query: "Why did God desire to send an angel before Moses?" Moreover, what was the nature of the angel, or messenger? And what was his precise function? Each of these questions he then proceeds to answer.

The book is divided into twenty-five chapters. Of these, the first ten are devoted to the usual series of questions, or "doubts", enumerating the several difficulties which the Sacred Text might offer to the uninitiated reader, e.g. what was the position of Moses, *vis-à-vis* the angel, during the entire period preceding the entry into the Promised Land? Two further chapters discuss the problem how Moses could have subsisted on the top of the mountain for forty days and nights, without food or drink. Another asks: What was the *libnath ha-ŝappir* (A.V. "paved work of a sapphire stone"), which, according to Exod. xxiv, 10, the chosen men of Israel beheld on the top of Sinai? Then follow three chapters outlining the method pursued in the replies, whilst the rest of the book is occupied by those replies themselves. These are based upon a metaphysical, rather than a literal and straightforward exegesis. Among other authorities quoted is a commentary written by the poet Immanuel of Rome, in which the physical ordeal of Moses on the top of the mountain is explained on the assumption that he had gradually put off the mortal frailty of the flesh and assumed a spiritual character, approaching that of angelic beings. By virtue thereof, the Lawgiver, so it was argued, was able to attain that high degree of intellectual perception which enabled him to receive the Law from God. Abravanel qualifies this view, but approves it in principle, and commends Immanuel for it. For his own part, he divides the forty days and nights into four equal periods, and enters into a minute description of the way in which Moses was slowly made to realize the mechanism of the Universe, the spiritual forces behind the movement of the spheres, etc., until at last, having been fully prepared, and having reached the highest peak of spiritual and intellectual development (to him identical) he was made worthy of receiving the Law for the second time.

'*Aṭereth Zeḳenim* was first published at Sabionetta in 1557, and subsequently reprinted at Amsterdam in 1739.

Zebaḥ Pesaḥ

From these semi-philosophical and semi-religious works of Abravanel, we now turn to those which seem to have constituted his chief activity during his stay at Monopoli. The '*Aṭereth Zeḳenim* was written in 1495, so that the next work would seem to be the *Zebaḥ Pesaḥ* (cf. Exod. xii, 27) written in 1496 and dealing with the service of the Passover. This has become the most popular of all Abravanel's writings, and it is written in a somewhat easier style than the others. The author does not here indulge in many philosophical speculations, although his mind now turns more and more passionately towards Messianic hopes and anticipations. In this

PLATE II

Illustrated Haggadah for Passover, with Abravanel's abbreviated commentary (*Ṣeli 'Esh*), Venice, 1629

The upper picture represents Israel's fertility (Exod. 1, 7), the lower one, the treasure cities (*ib.* 11).

commentary, past and future "blend and blur" in one unending continuity, and he sees in the various events of the past the pattern of those to follow in later ages. The Exodus from Egypt is the prototype for that from Spain. He promises to dwell upon it much more fully in later writings, and to deal therein with these problems exclusively, but here it is so clearly stated, almost in every portion of the Passover Service, that he cannot do otherwise in his commentary than expatiate on the events of the past and the outlook for the future. Although, in the printed edition, the division is not indicated, in the table of contents the author divides the text into 100 chapters or "gates", and with his usual dexterous application of biblical verses refers for explanation thereof to Gen. XXVI, 12, where it is said: "And Isaac sowed in that year and reaped 100 measures." The word for "measures" in the Bible is she'arim, plural of sha'ar, but this word also means "chapter", and Abravanel, therefore, interprets the text to mean that Isaac, i.e. himself, "assembled" 100 chapters. The work follows the usual form. He starts by raising problems and difficulties, and in a very long and prolix commentary proceeds to set all doubts at rest. The Haggadah known to Abravanel, like that of the Sephardim of to-day, ends with the Hallel. Evidently in his time all the poems which are found in the other rites were unknown. Among the questions he asks are, for example: Why the four sons in the Haggadah are not ranged in the order in which they are found in the Bible; Why the numerous miracles which are said to have happened at the Red Sea, are introduced into the Haggadah. He shows throughout a keen eye for possible problems and a delight in answering them. This book has been printed and reprinted over and over again, and, in view of its bulk, one edition, published by Judah di Modena in 1629, actually curtailed it, under the title Șeli 'Esh (Roasted in Fire) (cf. Exod. XII, 8). It has been printed, together with the Haggadah, as one of the most important commentaries.

Zebaḥ Pesaḥ shows a tendency towards pure homily, the author himself styling it Derush, i.e. Homiletical Exposition.

This tendency is, however, notably eschewed on those occasions whereon he prefers to indulge his philosophical proclivities or to adopt astrological interpretations. Thus, in one passage he goes so far as to identify the Paschal Lamb with the Constellation Aries (the Ram), seeking to prove an intimate connection between the two! Even these eccentricities, however, have not detracted from the favour in which the book has continued to be held.

The tragic course of events in Spain now began to show their traces in the literary and scholastic development of Abravanel. His mind turned ever and again to the remarkable parallelism between the Exodus from Egypt and that from Spain. Filled, on the one hand, with deep bitterness and resentment at the misfortunes which had overtaken his brethren, there was yet kindled in him, on the other, the fire of a fanatical passion and an ardent yearning for the speedy advent of the Messiah, with its promise of final release and redemption. At length, the strange parallelism of past and present events became with him an obsession, and the flames of desire burst into a blaze of indomitable belief. From this time forward, the mingling of despair and hope dominates his writing and comes into full expression.

Naḥalath 'Aboth

Still dwelling in retirement at Monopoli, Abravanel found a medium for this revolution of feeling in a commentary on that tractate of the Mishnah known as the "Ethics of the Fathers". Of all the products of post-biblical Hebrew literature none has been so often printed, commented upon and translated as these six chapters of ethical apophthegms and moral reflections, containing also a very slender chain of tradition. One can count the editions and translations almost by the hundred. From Maimonides to modern times, there is scarcely a single scholar of eminence who has not sought to interpret or translate the "Ethics". It is prized so highly that it has even been introduced into the liturgy, and on certain Sabbaths of the year consecutive chapters are read during the afternoon service, by way of ethical discourse designed to inculcate high principles of religious life and moral conduct. No wonder that Abravanel should also have sought to try his hand at the task. The result is an exhaustive commentary entitled *Naḥalath 'Aboth* (*The Inheritance of the Fathers*) (cf. Prov. xix, 14). The work was intended to be a kind of religious guide to his third and youngest son Samuel, to whom it is dedicated in a glowing introduction, expressing the hope that this son will follow in the footsteps of his father and learn to appreciate the value of this precious gift.

To a certain extent Samuel did indeed fulfil these expectations, for although he did not attain any great degree of Hebrew learning, yet he deserved his title *Nasi*. He inherited his father's financial capabilities, and amassing a considerable fortune, emulated him in his liberality and in the open-handed assistance which he rendered to the poor, especially to scholars. Moreover, he made his house a recognized rendezvous for the *intelligentsia* of the day.

As a prelude to the book proper, the *Naḥalath 'Aboth* carries a dedicatory poem addressed, in the name of the volume itself, to the reader, the author being Judah, the eldest son of Abravanel. It shows him a master of the Hebrew language and no less skilful than his father in adapting words and sentences from the Bible to his purpose. The acrostic is composed of his name, Judah son of Isaac, but in one of the last few lines he gives a curious transcript of the family name. It is written in three Hebrew words which read *Bar ben el*, to which is added the expression "son of Jesse", pointing to the Davidic origin of the family. Read as written, the name would be *Barbenel*, the translation being "son of the son of God", a very curious derivation and one open to the gravest misinterpretation.[1]

Then follow two introductions, and after these each sentence

---

[1] I have been told that among the officers now fighting at Bilbao one or more are called by the name Barbanel, a very remarkable coincidence with the above spelling of the name. I have not been able yet to discover the authenticity of this information which, however, I have no reason to doubt, since it was given to me spontaneously by a friend who said he had read it in one of the English newspapers.

found in the Chapters of the Fathers is taken *seriatim* and made
the subject of a very long commentary. This differs very
considerably from the aforementioned *Zebaḥ Pesaḥ*. Abravanel
is here not so much obsessed by the idea of the redemption,
and he displays an extraordinary erudition in trying to read
into the Bible much that does not lie on the surface, in order
to find the source of and the justification for these rabbinic
apophthegms. Moreover, he does not indulge to any great
degree in metaphysical or eschatological interpretations, nor
is he led away by astrological calculations.

Before embarking upon the commentary, Abravanel traces
the chain of tradition from Moses down to Judah the Prince,
compiler of the Mishnah. Here he shows himself in his best
strain, being very systematic and, like a financier, endeavour-
ing to put everything into very proper order. He covers the
whole period by four groups of names, each consisting of
twelve, the first beginning with Moses, the second beginning
with the Prophets, the third with Ezra, and the fourth with
Sanhedrin. In each of these groups he mentions not only the
names of the leading authorities but also their several contemporaries, especially in the later period. The reason for so
doing is that he wishes to point out that though single names
are mentioned in the Chapters of the Fathers, the sentences
do not comprise everything that they had to say, nor were
these the only men to preserve the tradition and transmit it
to their successors. On the contrary, they were merely the
more prominent men of each period, and they had a large
number of contemporaries, many of them very greatly
distinguished by their learning and equally cognizant of the
tradition which they shared with their masters. These contemporaries would, in their turn, also have been able to
preserve the tradition and hand it on to *their* successors. The
chain is, therefore, not limited to individuals, but extends to
entire groups, thus attesting the validity and importance of
the tradition. Given as he is to making comparisons between
past and present and between various phases or stages of
Jewish history, Abravanel here compares Moses with Ezra,
both being especially connected with the transmission of the

sacred Scriptures, and both having to fulfil a more or less similar role. Moses gave the Law to people going out of Egypt, and Ezra to a people who had come from just such another exile in Babylon. Moses is credited not only with having written the words of the Law but also with having established the *plene* and *defective* writing of them, and also those large and small letters found in the Pentateuch, since often legal deductions depended largely upon the actual orthography! Ezra, on his side, is said to have added accents, vowels and the division of verses. Abravanel explains further that he intends to show that the Sayings of the Fathers were not merely ethical precepts, as stated by Maimonides and others, but that they were religious principles rooted in the words of the Bible, and that they also possessed an internal sequence. Just as in every other tractate of the Mishnah there was an inner co-relation between one statement and the next, so in this there was an internal connection which had hitherto escaped attention. And not only was there such a close connection between the several sentences but also between the several chapters. Although in the later chapters of the tractate the biblical basis may seem to be less apparent, it is nevertheless present, and the entire work is regulated by a rigorous discipline of method. In his commentary, therefore, Abravanel adopts a deliberately simple style, and he calls the answers which he gives to the questions raised by him *Limmudin*, i.e. teachings. Here, by way of example, is the beginning of his commentary:

The text reads: "Moses received the Law from Sinai and transmitted it to Joshua, and Joshua to the Elders, the Elders to the Prophets, and the Prophets to the Men of the Great Synagogue." This reads very simply, but to Abravanel it is full of difficulties. In the first place: Why does it say that Moses received the Law from Sinai, seeing that he did not receive it from Sinai, but from God? Again: Why does it not say that he received it *on* Sinai or *in* Sinai, rather than *from* Sinai? Or again: Why did Joshua not transmit it to the High Priest Eleazar whom he had to consult on all matters of Law? How could Joshua have transmitted it to the Elders (in the plural) seeing that these continued for many generations? He could, at most, have transmitted it to *one* Elder, not to *all*. Further: Why did the Elders not transmit it to the King or to the High Priest instead of to the Prophets? etc., etc.

This commentary has also enjoyed great popularity. It appeared for the first time at Constantinople in 1505, during its author's lifetime. It was later reprinted three or four times in full (e.g. Constantinople, 1505; Venice, 1545 and 1546) and a few more times in abbreviated form.

Retired in Monopoli and brooding over the troubles which he had witnessed, Abravanel now turned more and more to the task of seeking comfort and consolation for himself and his brethren during that time of dire distress. With a zeal, a fire of conviction and a deep attachment to every word of the Holy Writ, he proceeded to compose three further works dealing exclusively with the expectation of final deliverance. Deeply convinced that the words of the Law contain more than appears on the surface, he endeavoured to delve into the very profundity of their meaning, reading into them, in an almost fantastic manner, interpretations and explanations discernible only by a keen mind like his own, trained in philosophical speculations. Mathematician as he was, and combining a rare gift for figures with a profound belief in astrology, he could see in the movement of the stars and in their various conjunctions portents of the future. A book, therefore, like that of Daniel, was like a heavenly gift to him. To him Daniel was a prophet, and with all his skill and knowledge he threw himself into the interpretation of his apocalyptic visions and into reading the riddle of those figures at the end of the book which had been the object of so many speculations and vain disappointments. Scholars had long endeavoured to find in them the exact date of the advent of the Messiah and the deliverance from that *Galuth* (*diaspora*) which now covered not only the Exile or dispersion but all the trials, persecutions and terrors to which the Jews had been subjected in so many lands for so many ages, and redemption from which had now perforce to combine spiritual and physical, economic and political aspects. Moreover, because of its apocalyptic contents the book of Daniel had been commented upon by Christian scholars with the especial intention of proving Jesus to be the Messiah and of deducing from other passages in the Bible the reason for the Jewish dispersion, as being in the nature of a punishment for their attitude towards the founder of Christianity.

Ma'ayene Hay-Yeshu'ah

Abravanel realized the fallacy of all such arguments and did not hesitate to demonstrate with unrelenting vigour, yet with a strong conviction, that they had all been misled. Although it is very difficult to follow him in the interpretation of these visions, one cannot but admire the skill of his arguments, and, above all, his passionate love for his people, or follow with sympathy his enthusiastic description of the future redemption and of the glorified Israel which he beheld in his dreams. The title of the book is *Ma'ayene Hay-yeshu'ah* (*The Wells of Salvation*) (cf. Isa. XII, 3), and this led him to apply the verse in Num. XXXIII, 9, where it is said: "And in Elim were twelve fountains of water and threescore and ten palm-trees." He therefore divided his book into twelve chapters which he called *fountains*, or *wells*, and these, in turn, he subdivided into *palms* or *palm trees* to the number of seventy. One cannot help admiring the skill of his exegesis; at the same time one is surprised to find him relying to such an extent on astrological calculations as to determine precisely the Advent of the Messiah and the beginning of the redemption for the year 1532 or 1533 (for as he says, a year more or less makes no difference). Nor this alone. He even goes so far as to affirm that he knew that one year before the expulsion from Spain the Messiah had already been born, i.e. in the year 1491, so convinced was he of the accuracy of his calculations. These rested on the comparison between the Exodus from Egypt— always a starting-point with him—and the Exodus from Spain. He worked out to his satisfaction that they had both taken place under the same great conjunction of the stars in the zodiacal sign of Pisces. This constellation was, therefore, according to him, the most favourable to Israel.

I am giving a specimen of the way in which Abravanel contrived to find justification for his calculations and hopes, by translating a portion of his interpretation of Ps. xc. This is not mysticism, nor is it mere allegory. It represents a definite system of exegesis, based on the conviction that the *ipsissima verba* of Scripture, especially in the case of the Pentateuch, the Prophets, the Book of Psalms and Daniel, were divinely inspired and that more is implied in them than can be deduced from a merely literal translation. Abravanel was struck by the fact that, according to the superscription of this Psalm, Moses uttered a prayer. Why, he asks, should Moses have prayed? What was his purpose? Surely it had reference to something connected with the future of Israel, and if so, what? He therefore endeavoured to find the purpose of the prayer, and he gives us the following explanation:

Since, according to his calculation, the great conjunction in Pisces would be identical with the same conjunction at the Exodus, he says that from the birth of Moses to the time of the Exodus 83 years have passed. Moses had been born three years before the conjunction, as he was 80 years old when he stood before Pharaoh. Now, the same number of years ought to pass from the persecution in Spain to the Redemption, so that the latter should take place in the year 1532 or 1533. It is possible, however, by the will of God, to hasten the time of redemption and to reduce the 80 years to 70 years, and that is what Moses says in his prayer (Ps. xc, 10): "The days of our years are threescore years and ten; even though in their full strength they (should) be fourscore years...." Thus, by the will of God, 70 years instead of 80 years would be the space of time between the birth of the Messiah and the Redemption. Similarly, the words (v. 1) "in generation and generation" (so the Hebrew literally), refers to the *two* generations of the conjunction which occurs twice within 3000 years, viz. (a) the generation of the redemption from Egypt, and (b) the generation of the future redemption. Moreover, the preservation of the Jewish nation transcends the ordinary rules of nature. It is to this that Moses refers in verse 2: "Before the mountains were created." This means that just as at the Creation God had been able to work with the absolute power (for which reason He is called "God"), so would He do also at the time of the future Redemption. Thus also the expression (v. 2) "from world to world" (translated in our Bible "from eternity unto eternity") refers to the two occurrences of this celestial conjunction, viz. (a) the birth of Moses, and (b) that of the Messiah. This Moses explains by saying (v. 3): "Thou turnest man to *crushing*", i.e. God will first crush Israel in the *Galuth*, as formerly in Egypt, and then, "return", i.e. and He promises that He will "return" to redeem them a second time. Moreover, Moses even reveals the length of this *Galuth*, for he says (v. 4): "a thousand years in thy sight are but as yesterday." Abravanel proceeds:

Behold the day consists of twenty-four hours and therefore the *Galuth* will be a full day, i.e. one thousand years. Moreover, it will continue until the "watch of the night", i.e. not until day-break but only until the first watch, which is in the middle of the night. And since the night is half of the day, this therefore denotes 500 years. Hence, the total length of the *Galuth* will be 1500 years, incomplete, for it will not be a complete night. This agrees entirely with what I have elsewhere shown, viz. that we have now continued for 1427 years in the *Galuth* of Rome. Therefore the time of the Redemption will be before 1500. It is for this reason that Moses says (v. 5): "Thou carriest them away as with a flood."

This refers to the *Galuth* under Titus. Moreover, he compares it also with "a sleep", and further with the sprouting of plants. This last is explained by such passages as Ps. xcii, 14: "they will still be green in their old age" or Job xiv, 7: "there is hope for the tree", and it is in this sense that Moses here compares Israel with the "grass which groweth up" and which "flourisheth in the morning, though in the evening it be cut down and wither". Such, indeed, is the state of our people during the *Galuth*. Further, when Moses uses the expression "in the morning", he is referring to the era of the First and Second Temples, and when he says "in the night it is cut down" he is referring to the present *Galuth*. And since he affirms a full "day" consists of a thousand years, the time when the sun is actually shining upon the earth (being only the half) is 500 years, and this is the time appointed for each of the two Temples which indeed existed close upon 500 years each. Moreover, Moses does not take into account that short spell of the Exile in Babylon, but refers directly to that longer *Galuth* which now obtains, when he says: "in the evening it will be cut down and wither." "Cut down" refers to the destruction of the First Temple and "wither" to that of the Second. Accordingly, Moses continues (vv. 7, 8), "we are consumed by thine anger and by thy wrath are we troubled. Thou hast set our iniquities before thee". Yet, since we have been punished for sins, he adds at once: "and our secret sins in the light of thy countenance". Abravanel continues:

I believe that this refers to the future redemption, viz. to the second occurrence of the conjunction which will coincide with the birth-pangs of the Messianic Age. Where there was previously obscuration and gloom, i.e. the darkness of oppression, there will at last arise the light of the Redemption. Therefore Moses prays that God may regard those times of tribulation, and cause them speedily to end, since we have already suffered so much. "Our days have been consumed in thy wrath" says Moses, as if to declare: "What we have already suffered in the *Galuth* is enough; therefore increase not our tribulation in this time of our servitude." Thereupon he explains how long this time of servitude will last, for he says: "the days of our years are threescore years and ten", meaning thereby that it need not necessarily continue for a full 80 years, but might be curtailed to 70, though at the most it cannot be more than 80, even as it was in the time of Moses. And Moses points out that during those years the tribulations will, in fact, be increased, for he says: "in their full complement (strength) is trouble and sorrow." Nevertheless, when the appointed season arrives, matters will be hastened, for it is also said (v. 10), "but it is soon cut off, and we fly away". This means that if God wills to make the time shorter than it was in Egypt, we will rise up in greatness and honour and will soar like the birds athwart the heavens. Since, however, he did not know for certain the number of the years of servitude, he adds: "Who knoweth the power of thine anger?" i.e. there is no certain knowledge as to how long the "birth-pangs" of the Messianic Age will continue. The text continues: "And according to thy fear, so is thy wrath." This means that the length of the tribulations will be determined by the extent of the fear with which the people regard God.

Finally, Abravanel concludes by remarking that the precise date has never been revealed, in order that the people should not be led astray and afterwards lose their hope of the final redemption, should that time pass and nothing happen. Yet, he adds, in spite of his own assertion:

None the less, I know for sure that the Messiah has already been born, since this increased persecution and oppression are signs that we have entered the period of the "birth-pangs" of the Messiah, prior to his ultimate appearance which is sure to be soon, in the year which I calculated above, viz. 1532.

This extract will suffice to illustrate the manner in which Abravanel interprets the verses of the Bible. He continues in the same style for the rest of the Psalm.

It is interesting to notice that he discusses the anti-Christ legend, of which Christian scholars had made sorry use in their commentaries, as well as many other statements which he found scattered in their works. In his speculations concerning the Last Day, he points scornfully to his predecessors, declaring roundly that they have misled the people by false calculations, already refuted by the fact that the dates predicted by them had already passed. Unfortunately, the same fate has overtaken his own calculations and this has practically sealed the fate of his work. Nevertheless, it has not altogether outlived its usefulness, for there is still gold to be found among the dross, and the underlying desire to unravel the mysteries of the Daniel apocalypse is one which is at least praiseworthy. *Ut desint vires, tamen est laudanda voluntas.*

Maʿayene Hay-Yeshuʿah was composed at Monopoli in 1497; it seems to have exercised also a great influence later on, for others had only to alter the dates and find other conjunctions favourable to their own calculations, to utilize all the fundamental arguments adduced by Abravanel. It is unknown where and when the first edition appeared—no date is given in my copy—but I have reason to believe that it was printed in Salonica and possibly even in its author's lifetime. To suggest that it was printed in Naples seems to me to be erroneous, since, to my knowledge, no books appeared in Naples after 1492. If anywhere, Salonica or Constantinople would have been the place where such a book, intended to give comfort and hope to the stricken people, would have been printed. Ferrara, 1551, seems to be doubtful.

Mashmia 'Yeshu'ah

Ma'ayene Hay-Yeshu'ah was soon followed by Abravanel's *Mashmia 'Yeshu'ah* (*Announcer of Salvation*) (cf. Isa. LII, 7) written in Monopoli, between 1497 and 1498. Abravanel was not satisfied merely with the witness of Daniel to the advent of the Messiah, nor would it have been sufficiently satisfactory to the people who, as he writes in the introduction, had already lost all hope, more especially since some of the most reputable teachers had declared categorically that all prophetical utterances concerning the future of the Jewish people had already been fulfilled during the period of the Second Temple. These prophecies—so they had asserted— were not intended to declare anything referring to a future after the destruction of the Temple. Abravanel was afraid that many might be inclined to listen to the voice of those who, basing themselves upon such pronouncements, sought to beguile them into renouncing their ancient faith on the grounds that all things prophesied in it had long since come to an end and that it therefore held no hope for the present age. Moreover, a tendency had arisen, born out of hopelessness, to reject therewith all belief in references to the Resurrection of the Dead, the Day of Judgement, the Advent of the Messiah and the future Glory of Israel reunited in the old home. Abravanel therefore undertook to prove from the Bible the truth of those expectations. In so doing, he not infrequently stretches a point beyond reason, but his ingenuity never fails. There is little philosophical speculation and little astrology in this work, but much of that same extraordinary method of exegesis as is revealed in his interpretation of Daniel.

In seventeen chapters, the author assembles and discusses some sixty biblical passages bearing on the Resurrection of the Dead, the Last Day and the future Redemption, seeking thereby to show that each of these has indeed been foretold in Holy Writ. The work opens with an examination of the oracle of Balaam, and continues with four arguments from the Pentateuch, fifteen from Isaiah, seven from Jeremiah, ten from Ezekiel, a couple from the Minor Prophets, twelve from the Psalms and, curiously enough, only one from Daniel. In discussing the Psalms, Abravanel concentrates chiefly on those ascribed to the sons of Korah and to Asaph, finding therein predictions of future persecutions and trials, as well as of ultimate redemption and glory. When due allowance is made for the author's characteristic style of exegesis, with its markedly allegorical flavour, the work will be found to constitute a mine of interesting and curious information, whilst a certain vigour is imparted to it by the polemical strain in which Abravanel inveighs against those who would adopt a too literal and matter-of-fact interpretation of the texts.

Of especial interest is the fact that Abravanel regards the final song of Moses (Deut. XXXII, 1–43) as a prophetic utterance, and interprets the last six verses in an eschatological sense. This recalls the Samaritan interpretation, although there is, of course, no connection. The conception, however, is the same in both cases, viz. that the future destiny of Israel is foretold in that Song, including not only their punishment and that of the heathen, but also their final redemption. The work is said to have been printed at Salonica, in 1526, but I have not seen a copy of this *editio princeps*. A second edition appeared at Amsterdam (?), but neither the place of printing nor the name of the printer is to be found.

Yeshuʿōth Meshiḥō

One more work, probably the last, so far as is known, written by Abravanel before going to Venice, is also devoted to the same subject. It is entitled *Yeshuʿōth Meshiḥō* (*The Salvation of His Anointed*) (cf. Ps. XXVIII, 8). Abravanel had noted with surprise and regret that, especially when involved in forced public disputations with apostates, the Rabbis invariably confined themselves to answering the alleged arguments drawn from Scriptures but neglected to pay attention to legends and allusions found in rabbinical literature, i.e. in the Talmud and Midrash. He reproved this, as showing great weakness, for it afforded an opportunity for others to assert that the Rabbis were incapable of answering convincing arguments drawn from those sources. It therefore appeared to him necessary to bridge that gap, not only in order that such arguments should be refuted, but also in order to explain to his own people the true inwardness and meaning of these traditional legends.

Among those whom he praises for the admirable manner in which they had met such cases is Rabbi Solomon ben Adrat. Abravanel here refers, unquestionably, to the famous *Responsum* in which Solomon replies to an inquiry concerning the degree of credibility or faith to be attached to those many legends and apparent superstitions found in Talmud and Midrash, and the nature of their authority in point of Jewish law.[1] He then collects 150 passages, some shorter, some longer, from the Talmud and Midrash and gives his own explanations of them. Sometimes he is not satisfied with only one explanation but attempts two or three different ones, literal, allegorical, or philosophical. He finds fault, among others, with Naḥmanides, who, when involved in a disputation with the apostate Fra Paolo of Burgos and confronted with a certain legend, had no other answer to give than: legends and tales are of no legal value to us. The legend in question is that told in the Talmud[2] concerning a man who, whilst ploughing his field, was met by an Arab who told him: "Unyoke your oxen and remove the harness, for the Temple has just been destroyed; there is no future for thee and thy work on the soil." After a while, the same Arab came back and told him: "Yoke your oxen and resume your work, for

---

[1] This *Responsum*, by the way, is of such an admirable character that it would repay being reprinted to-day with an adequate translation and annotation.
[2] *J. Ber.* ii, § 4, f. 5 *a*, line 12.

the Messiah has just been born and will restore the freedom of the Jews." When asked where he was born, the Arab said: "In Bethlehem of Judah." The man then left his plough and went to find the child. He discovered the mother and the child in a state of great poverty. He bought for the child the swaddling-clothes, which the mother could not afford, and after a time came back again to see what had happened to the child. The mother told him that demons and spirits had carried it away. The application of this legend to the birth of Jesus is too obvious not to have been utilized by the disputant in order to confound the Rabbi. Abravanel then explains it, in the first place, by saying that very likely the Messiah had been born, but what appeared to the woman to have been demons and evil spirits that had carried it away were in fact angels who had taken the child and carried it to Paradise, since the time for redemption had not yet come. The Messiah is still waiting for the time when he is to appear. However, Abravanel is not satisfied with this single interpretation, so adds a second and a third.

Yeshu'oth Meshihô was entirely lost until Rabbi David Sinzheim of Paris discovered it in his library and handed it over to the brothers Bisliches, who undertook the publication of it. To all intents and purposes they were also its editors, for the author had omitted to indicate where, in Talmud and Midrash, the various legends discussed were to be found. This omission was rectified by them, the reference being given to each item in the table of contents. The book was printed for the first and only time in Carlsruhe, 1838. It is divided into three parts, each containing four chapters subdivided into a number of paragraphs of unequal length. The index at the beginning does not indicate the chapters, but refers to the passage from the legends and sentences from Talmud and Midrash of a Messianic character, discussed and interpreted by Abravanel.

Whether this was indeed the last book written by Abravanel and whether, in fact, all his writings have been published, it is impossible to say with certainty. A strange fate seems to have overtaken his manuscripts. It was mere chance that his commentary on the *Guide of the Perplexed* should have been discovered as late as the beginning of last century, after more than 300 years, in a late copy made in Tunis.[1] It may be, on the other hand, that his activity in Venice again prevented him from continuing his literary work.

The Influence of Abravanel

It is difficult to estimate the importance of Abravanel's literary career and the influence he has exercised on succeeding generations.

With his death there comes to a close one of the golden ages of Jewish poetry, philosophy and biblical scholarship. His genius may be regarded, indeed, as the last rays of a setting sun, to be followed by a period of unrelieved darkness and obscurity. Paradoxical as it may sound, the Middle Ages begin for Jewish history with the commencement of the sixteenth century. Whereas in the rest of the world, and especially in Italy, the flower of the Renaissance was then bursting into blossom, over the Jews hung the pall of thick darkness and the shadow of death. Driven from pillar to post, expelled now from Frankfurt, now from Prague and now from Vienna, robbed and decimated in the Thirty Years' War, massacred later in Poland and the Ukraine, their sorry and insecure existence scarcely induced that ease of spirit in which cultural achievement is alone possible. The stress of life brought their arts to a sudden end, and the scholar's lamp shed its tiny glow only in one or other remote corner of the Exile. On the other hand, born out of very despair and out of the desire to find, at all costs, some basis upon which present disasters might be reconciled with a belief in divine justice and present calamities with an undying hope in future restoration, there arose a marked tendency to fall back upon mystical speculations and esoteric philosophies. These slowly begin to fill the place of an earlier rationalism and literalism whose conclusions had not to encounter the conflict of im-

[1] From that copy Landau printed it for the first time, and it was then reprinted in the Warsaw edition of the *Guide*, along with the two other commentaries of 'Ephodi and Shemtob.

mediate circumstances. It is no exaggeration to say that what the Bible had been to their grandfathers, the Zohar now became to the people at large. Little understood, but essentially mystical and esoteric, it furnished them at once with a higher authority, in the light of whose teachings they might assess their present woes.

Out of this tendency towards mysticism there later arose the Kabbalistic system associated with the name of Luria. Theories of Metempsychosis and spiritual exaltation provided a convenient escape-mechanism from the grimmer realities of economic hardship, which men might then be content to regard as the necessary "Dark Night" of mystical experience. Moreover, here was fertile soil upon which the seeds of Messianic hope might well be sown, and out of which Messianic movements might well flourish. It is possible, indeed, that Abravanel's own writings fostered these dreams.

But there was another side to this picture, and it is one which might indeed be illustrated by the experience of our own day. Whilst, on the one side, there were those who were engaged, above all things, in seeking to reconcile Jewish hopes with immediate actualities, and therefore resorted to mysticism for the solution of the riddle, there were, on the other, large communities so immersed in the struggle for existence that they simply had not the time for such religious preoccupations. To them, the more immediate necessity was not to formulate an inspiriting doctrine of Jewish destiny, but to determine the regimen of Jewish life upon traditional principles. Examination of Talmudic law, often entailing even minute points of disputation, were to them more important than general philosophies, so that for Abravanel and his form of thought they had little time, and he tended to become outmoded.

Nevertheless, for some little while at least, and due to the filial piety of his sons, the influence of Abravanel seems to have continued in more cultured circles. At Ferrara, the Duke of Este had granted the Jews freedom of life and work, and there also Donna Gracia Mendes had taken up her abode and the Usques family flourished. It is possible that

in such favourable surroundings, where economic pressure
was not so insistent, the influence of Abravanel lived on for
one or two generations. It may be a mere shot in the dark,
but I think it is at least worth suggesting that the first
Spanish translation of the Bible by Abraham Usque was
directly due to that influence. Abravanel had laid so much
stress on the necessity of studying the Bible, on the deep
meaning, and the great comfort which that study would
bring, that it is easy to understand why the Spanish translation should have been published at just that time. There
were, no doubt, many of the refugees who were not conversant
with Hebrew, but who were nevertheless anxious to know
something more of their own great treasure. Without some
express stimulus from without, it would be difficult to understand why they should undertake such a great work as that
of the translation.[1]

But still more directly do I see the influence of Abravanel's
description of the great future awaiting the Jews, in the last
chapter of Samuel Usque's *Consolations for the Tribulations of
the House of Israel*, which appeared in Ferrara in 1552. He
describes there, in singularly glowing terms, the great future
which awaits the reunited and free Israel in the Land of their
Fathers—a poetic vision which could not fail to impress the
reader and bring him true consolation.[2]

Whilst Abravanel's works, especially the biblical commentaries and philosophic treatises, remained practically
ignored and forgotten by the Jews, their publication coincided not only with the Renaissance but even, more signifi-
cantly, with the Reformation. The Bible became the object

[1] The book appeared in two recensions, the second with a slight change in
Isaiah (vii, 14) where, instead of *moza*, "the young woman", the word *virgen*,
"maid", had been substituted to satisfy Christian interpretation and to obtain
the approval of the Inquisition; an otherwise identical edition appeared in the
same year. For the rest it remained the same. This became the standard Bible
of the Spanish Jews, especially in the West, but also in the East. The Pentateuch
was reproduced in the Constantinople 1546 edition, where the Spanish letters
were reproduced in Hebrew type, and the whole at Salonica, in 1568, and then
over and over again, in whole or in parts.

[2] I possess in my library a manuscript of the translation made into English
by E. H. Lindo and the Introduction and first few chapters in a revised form have
been published by me in the *Jewish Forum* of New York.

of intensive study on the part of Christian scholars, since the Reformation turned chiefly upon a proper understanding and interpretation of the Hebrew text. A number of Hebraists then arose who studied the Hebrew language and wrote in Hebrew, and many Hebrew works were translated into Latin. The attention of these scholars was thus drawn to the works of Abravanel. We find a large number of them translating or excerpting from them, or attacking Abravanel. Foremost among them is Buxtorf junior, who was one of the first to add some excerpts from Abravanel's writings to his Latin translation of the *Cuzari*—a book which is in itself a philosophic apology for Judaism. I can mention here only a few more prominent names, Lakemacher, Alting, L'Empereur, all of whom comment on various passages of Abravanel's biblical commentaries, Hulsius, and Carpzov on Daniel, and a good many on his commentary on Jonah. Surenhuis incorporated a translation of *Naḥalat 'Aboth* into his Latin translation of the Mishna, whilst, in 1712, J. H. Mai translated *Mashmia' Yeshu'ah*, adding thereto a biography of Abravanel.

It is always difficult to assess the influence which a man's writings may have exercised upon his own generation, but there cannot be much doubt that the feverish Messianic hopes which animated the contemporaries of Abravanel and his immediate successors must have been fed by the passionate expectation of the advent of the Messiah and the redemption from persecution within the next thirty years expressed so forcibly by Abravanel in his various writings. It is also possible that these may have contributed towards stirring up the hopes aroused by the appearance of the mysterious David Reubeni, and towards furnishing fuel for the ecstatic enthusiasm of Solomon Molho and all who at that time were given to dream of and to hope for the end of the *Galuth* and the beginning of a new era of freedom. True, great disappointment followed these exaggerated expectations, but no limit of time or space could be put to the workings of the spirit, and the hope of a Messianic redemption could not be extinguished altogether from the heart of the people. We find the first trace of it in the next century, again among the

Sephardic communities, notably at Amsterdam. There the works of Abravanel were reprinted, and these doubtless helped to kindle the new enthusiasm. Its most prominent exponent in that city was Manasseh ben Israel, who, by the way, married an Abravanel. One of his most important works was the *Conciliador*, written in Spanish, and printed at Amsterdam in 1639 ("Frankfort" on the title-page is a mere blind).[1] In every stage of his argument, and passage by passage, he refers to Abravanel and uses his arguments to reconcile apparent contradictions and difficulties in the text of the Bible. Even in later times, the influence of this work and of Abravanel can be seen in the commentary of David Levi to the Bible.

Manasseh ben Israel's work under the title *Piedra gloriosa*, or *The Glorious Stone* (on the statue erected by Nebuchadnezzar) contains an interpretation of the Book of Daniel which can be understood and studied only in connection with Abravanel's book on Daniel. No less great was the influence of Abravanel on Manasseh ben Israel's work on the *Resurrection of the Dead*. All these topics are derived from the writings of Abravanel, and are inspired by them. Far more important, however, for the ultimate career of Manasseh, was his work *The Hope of Israel*, published in Amsterdam, 1650. This also stands under the inspiring influence of Abravanel. It was this work which directly contributed to the readmission of the Jews into England. Moreover, the Messianic hopes kindled and fortified by Manasseh's writings and traceable to Abravanel, have prepared a fertile soil for many pseudo-Messianic movements, culminating in the appearance of *Sabbatai Zebi*. It was in 1659 that this booklet was reprinted in Smyrna, just at the height of this pseudo-Messianic movement, and it no doubt contributed to the success of it.

Indirectly, no doubt, the philosophic speculations of Abravanel, born of ardent love for his people, may have had a deep influence on his gifted son, Leone Hebreo. Father and son lived on most intimate terms, and the profound appreciation of his father's work and thought has found expression

[1] The work was translated into English by E. H. Lindo in 1842.

in a dedicatory poem and in other writings of his son. How much of the neo-Platonism which distinguished the great work of Leone is due to the inspiration of his father can only be appreciated after an intensive study of his works, notably those portions in which he speaks of the great love of God for his people and even of the great love of God for the world, His Creation. Leone Hebreo was in need of comfort, for he was indeed a "man of sorrow, acquainted with grief". A son of his had been kidnapped, baptized, and retained in Portugal, and this proved a lifelong source of grief to him. Renowned as a physician, he was still greater as the author of the famous *Dialoghi di amore* where he caught the first rays of the Renaissance, to which he contributed impressively by that great poem on love universal.[1] Apart from its contents, the beautiful Italian style in which that book is composed has earned the admiration of all readers. Indeed, it has sometimes been wondered how he could in so short a while have acquired the elegance and polish of that style, seeing that he left Spain with his father in 1492 and wrote the *Dialoghi* in 1502. If one may venture to express the idea that the work was, in fact, translated by a Christian friend from another language, say Spanish or Portuguese, into Italian, this would also explain some of those perplexing passages which have given rise to controversy as to whether Leone remained steadfast in his Judaism or not. It is scarcely credible that he should have changed his faith, in view of the tragedy of which he was himself a witness and victim. Had he such inclination he could easily have remained with his baptized son and he would not have written such glowing Hebrew poems as he did as late as 1498. It is clear that he preferred the exile, and the company of his father, to share with him and his fellow-sufferers the trials and tribulations of his chequered life.

This contention rests on the following fact. I have in my possession an old manuscript, which I have reason to believe

[1] Incidentally, I should like to remark that the first edition of the *Dialoghi* appeared after the death of Leone, "Leone" being the Italian translation of his full name Aryeh, the cognomen of Yehudah. Judah is described in the blessing of Jacob as the lion (cf. Gen. XLIX).

is contemporary, in which the *Dialoghi* are written in Spanish, but with Hebrew characters. I know that three translations were indeed made into Spanish several years after the Italian edition appeared, but the language of these does not seem to correspond with that of my manuscript. There are, if I remember aright, corrections in it, and I question whether this is not a copy of Leone's Spanish original and written with Hebrew characters. It is unlikely that anyone would have taken the Italian text, translated it into Spanish or Portuguese and written it in Hebrew characters. Again, if he had made a copy from the Spanish translation, being fully versed in the Spanish language and script, what interest would he have had in writing it in Hebrew characters? It would be quite another matter, however, if the original had been written in that language *in Hebrew characters*, and if from it the Italian translation had been made by some person who was not a Jew and who did not hesitate to insert those doubtful passages which have given rise to so much argument.

At the same time Abravanel also lives on as the hero of a legend, for he has impressed himself on the poetic memory of his people.

A legend originally connected with Maimonides, but belonging, in fact, to the general popular literature of the world and finding its counterpart among many nations, has been transferred to Abravanel. It appears in the Hebraeo-Arabic work *Ma'ase Sha'ashu'im*, and the full list of parallels has been given in my *Exemplar of the Rabbis*, No. 345, p. 246. The legend reads as follows:

Abravanel was held in high honour by the King whom he served, and it was his duty to bring the King (Sultan) a new Kaftan and a pair of slippers every Friday (the Sabbath of the Mohammedans). This aroused the jealousy of the Vizier, who thereupon repaired to the cobbler and asked him to insert into the sole of the slippers a piece of paper with the name of Mohammed written upon it. He then went to the King and said: "Abravanel not only hates our faith, but he also insults the name of the Prophet, placing it in the sole of your slipper that you should trample upon it." As proof of this assertion he ripped open the sole and showed the King the slip of paper with the name of Mohammed written upon it. Thereupon the King grew furious, and ordered the steward in charge of the royal oven to heat it for three days and to cast into it the man who would come and ask: Have you done the King's orders? On the third day, he sent for Abravanel. On the way a Jew stopped him, asking him to come and complete the *Minyan* (religious quorum) at the circumcision of his son. Abravanel went with him and stayed till the end of the ceremony. Meanwhile the Vizier, losing patience, had gone to the steward in charge of the oven and asked whether he had fulfilled the King's command. Immediately, the steward seized him and cast him into the oven. Abravanel came later, and was told by the steward that he had fulfilled the King's order. When Abravanel returned to the King, the latter, greatly astonished, asked what had happened and found out the truth, whereupon Abravanel was held in even higher honour.

And now, after so many centuries, Abravanel is again coming slowly into his own. He stands out as the prominent figure at the crossing of the ways; he has left a rich inheritance for those who will be willing to gather it, and his name has been written with golden letters in the history of the Jewish people. And at the present day, when a further tragic chapter is being written in the history of the Jews, he furnishes an heroic example of passionate love for his people and unabated faith in the ultimate advent of the Messiah and the final redemption from the *Galuth*.

Lecture IV

ABRAVANEL AS EXEGETE

BY DR L. RABINOWITZ

The following editions of Abravanel's Commentaries have been used:

Pentateuch, Hanover, 1710.

Early Prophets, Second Edition, 1686; no place mentioned.

Later Prophets, Second Edition, 1641, no place mentioned.

ABRAVANEL AS EXEGETE

DON ISAAC ABRAVANEL was first and foremost a biblical commentator and exegete. For nearly half a century he laboured on his commentaries on the Pentateuch, on the earlier and later prophets, and on his *Ma'yene hay-Yeshu'ah*, which is but a Messianic commentary on Daniel, and, with few and relatively unimportant exceptions, his other works grew consciously out of his main preoccupation, as branches from a parent trunk. Thus *'Atereth Zekenim* is a commentary on but one verse of the Bible (Exod. xxiii, 20), while his *Mashmia' Yeshu'ah* is but a "reprint", if the solecism may be permitted, of the relevant Messiological passages of his *magnum opus*. Biblical commentary was his *forte*, and to it he devoted the whole of the fruits of his massive intellect, his wide and extensive learning, his experience at the courts of kings.

There are two remarkable facts which emerge from a consideration of the chronology of Abravanel's works, both of which find their explanation in one basic assumption. The first is the amazing and almost phenomenal rapidity with which he committed his commentaries to writing. Thus, despite the fact that verbosity and digressiveness are his besetting sins, he completed the committal to writing of his commentary on Joshua in sixteen days. Four days afterwards, he commenced that on Judges, which was completed twenty-four days later. Six days only were allowed to lapse, and two and a half months later saw the completion of his commentary on both books of Samuel, despite the fact that before he could sit down to write it, he had to study, for the first time in his life, the Book of Chronicles and take careful, meticulous and exhaustive note of the many discrepancies, major and minor, between the parallel accounts.

The second fact is the apparently fitful and desultory manner in which he wrote his commentaries. The first recension of his commentary on Deuteronomy was completed at the age of twenty. For twenty-four years he wrote nothing, and then, in less than four months, the commentaries on Joshua, Judges and Samuel were complete. Again he lays down his pen, to take it up eight years later to continue his commentary on Kings, and so on.

And yet this fitfulness is, as I say, only apparent, and it is easily explained. Such appears to have been Abravanel's devotion to the immediate task which he had in hand, that he could not engage in two pursuits simultaneously. When in the royal service, he did not write a word. Immediately circumstances freed him from this yoke, he worked at full pressure on his commentaries. Joshua, Judges and Samuel were written during the six months between his flight from Portugal in 1483 and his entry into the service of Ferdinand and Isabella in 1484. The gap of eight years is the period of this service, when his pen is idle. Immediately the exile from Spain freed him from this service, he took up his pen again.

Both these peculiarities, apparently contradictory, are susceptible of one and the same interpretation. He formed the idea of his commentary on the historical books during his early manhood, and during the whole period when he was in the royal service he was consciously and unconsciously preparing himself for his labour of love, by deep and wide reading, by keen observation of men and affairs, by the study of every work, both Jewish and non-Jewish, relevant to his task. The whole commentary was formed in his mind, and all he had to do was to commit it to writing. Nothing is more impressive than the manner in which he says "I will deal with this matter when I comment on such and such a passage", and although there may be a gap of twenty years between the intention and the execution, infallibly the promised comment is found in the appointed place. No more perfect example of lifelong devotion to a cherished dream and of its translation into reality can be found than in the execution by Abravanel of his biblical commentaries.

Abravanel, in one of his characteristic excursus with which I shall deal later, differentiates between the wisdom of Solomon and that of an ordinary man by stating that whereas

PLATE III

Abravanel's commentary on Deuteronomy, Sabbionetta, 1551.

The title of the commentary is *Mirkébeth ham-Mishneh* (Gen. XLI, 43).

Solomon's wisdom came to him complete overnight, other men acquire it only by dint of the task of learning, the fatigue of research, penetrating and eager insight, by practical experience, and by the passage of time. Each of these *desiderata* of learning was exemplified in Abravanel's own life. His industry was amazing, his knowledge positively phenomenal. It was based both upon deep and wide reading, and upon information gained at the courts of kings and from travellers. I think that a claim could be made out for Abravanel as one of the most learned men of his time, both in Hebrew and in secular knowledge, and a bare list of some of the authorities quoted by him is eloquent of his encyclopaedic knowledge.

Jewish sources are to him naturally an open book. Talmud and Midrash, Rashi, Ibn Ezra, David Ḳimḥi, Gersonides, Naḥmanides, Ibn Caspi among the commentators; Maimonides, Crescas and other philosophers; the Zohar and other Kabbalistic works; Benjamin of Tudela and hosts of others are all used by him. Nor does he ignore the Karaite commentators. But even more impressive is a list, by no means complete, of Greek, Roman, Christian and Mohammedan authors quoted by him. Pythagoras, Empedocles, Anaxagoras, Aristotle and Plato, Seneca, Ptolemy, Sallust and Virgil, Pliny, Plotinus, Porphyry, Galen and Hermes Trismegistus, Valerius Maximus, ancient Spanish historians, "the books of the Latins", the New Testament, Jerome, Augustus, the Venerable Bede and Sextus Julius Africanus, Isidore of Seville, Thomas Aquinas, Albertus Magnus, Nicholas de Lyra and others. John de Mandeville's travels are quoted by him by name, and on many occasions he refers to information gleaned from travellers and merchants.[1] With his commentary as one's sole source, one could draw up a pretty accurate and detailed account of early Persian, Greek and Roman history, of the birth of Christianity and its early history, and of the Christianization of the Roman Empire.

Nor is he content with the bare mention of his authorities, but it is characteristic of him that, especially in the case of his Jewish authorities, he sums up their virtues and their

[1] See Addenda, p. 92.

failings in a terse sentence, which is all the more striking in view of his definite tendency towards prolixity. Thus, although he refers[1] to Rashi as "the Holy Rabbi", and accords him due praise as the founder of the rational interpretation of Scripture, elsewhere[2] he says: "It is a source of sorrow and bitterness to me that Rashi contented himself, in the majority of cases, in his commentary on the Bible, with the homiletical interpretations of the Rabbis of the Talmud."

Although his reverence for Maimonides is extreme, he does not hesitate vigorously to attack him[3] when his predilection for squaring Divine Revelation with Aristotelian philosophy leads him astray: "How remote", he says in one passage,[4] "are those views of Maimonides from the truth according to the true Torah!...Would that I knew what he meant by it, and what was his intention in this passage." Of Ibn Ezra he says,[5] "But R. Abraham ibn Ezra scoffed at this, as is his wont, for he laps up scoffing like water." He makes constant use of Josephus' monumental work, but he is by no means deceived as to its accuracy in certain cases. "Many things", he writes,[6] "Josephus wrote which are the very reverse of the truth and in opposition to the Divine Record, in order to gain the favour of the Romans, as a slave who stands in the power of his harsh masters, and who is forced to do their bidding." David Ḳimḥi he attacks[7] rather unfairly for plagiarism. "That which he quotes in the name of his father is, in fact, taken from Ibn Ezra. Why did he have to steal?" And so on.

It is obvious from the above that Abravanel prides himself upon his originality, and it is a pride for which a study of his works provides a complete justification. As an exegete, especially of the purely historical books of the Bible, both in his methods and in the nature of his commentary he stands alone and without equal, and it is difficult to understand the latter-day neglect of him.

In his Introduction to Joshua, for all practical purposes the first of his commentaries, he sets out in detail both the

---

[1] On Isa. xxvi, 7.   [2] *Comm. on Joshua*, Introd.   [3] Cf. I Kings viii, 11.
[4] II Sam. xxiv, Introd. f. 184*d*.   [5] On Exod. xx, 2.
[6] *Ma'yene hay-Yeshu'ah* (cited as *M.Y.*) x, 7.   [7] *Comm. on Amos*, end.

method which he intended to adopt, and to which, incidentally, he rigidly adhered, and a comparison between his projected commentary and those of his predecessors. It is in this passage that he makes the above-mentioned criticism of Rashi, and declares his intention of avoiding his mistake. Ibn Ezra, he says, confined himself to the grammar of individual words, and to the superficial rational meaning, and in many cases, he says in criticism of him, his commentary is shorter than the verse itself! Others followed in his wake and interpreted Scripture as a book of history or as a secular song. "Ḳimḥi does not make use of *Midrashim*, but I will do so. I will not speak in riddles as do Ibn Ezra and Naḥmanides, nor will I deduce moral lessons, as does Gersonides, Scripture itself providing its own moral, but I will explain the verses as they appeal to me." And he concludes with one of his rare boasts, to the effect that a comparison between his work and those of his predecessors is sufficient to demonstrate which is the superior.

In this passage he raises prolixity and digressiveness to the level of a virtue. Of brief commentaries he says, "The brevity of their comments is but an indication of the brevity of their minds", and only on rare occasions does he say "I will not pursue this matter for fear of becoming too lengthy".[1]

His method is unique, and he can lay claim to being the founder of the science of biblical propaedeutics. He was the first to preface each book with a general introduction dealing with the character of the book, its author, the date of its composition, and a précis of its contents. He then divides the book into sections and—apart from the Pentateuch, where the "questions" are without fixed number—he prefaces each section with six questions, consisting of difficulties, inconsistencies and problems which arise therein, and he then proceeds with his exposition. The exposition is not verse by verse, but a free paraphrase of the biblical section, in the course of which he answers all the difficulties.

This peculiar method of prefacing each section with questions he appears to have borrowed from Alphonso Tostat

[1] Gen. x, 2, xi, 1, xx, 1.

(Bishop of Avila, 1414–54), and he states quite frankly that the questions are sometimes forced, their main purpose being merely to aid the memory, and they gave rise to a gibe which I have never seen in print, but which I heard in my youth. The difficulties he propounds are so convincing, and his solution of them is so unconvincing, that many students of Abravanel became heretics!

He is the first commentator to deal systematically with the discrepancies between parallel passages in the Bible, e.g. Samuel and Kings on the one hand, and Chronicles on the other, or between the song of David as found in II Sam. xxii and in Psalm xviii. He states explicitly that he is a pioneer in this.[1] "I am the only one to occupy myself with this. No one has written a word of this before. There is no commentary on Chronicles to be found in the whole of Spain, except for a few words of Ḳimḥi, nor is it studied in Spain, and I confess to my shame that I myself have never studied it until now." He carefully and methodically enumerates no less than seventy-four discrepancies between II Sam. xxiii and I Chron. xi, and proceeds to account for every single one of them.

But perhaps the greatest excellence of his commentary is the direct result of the exalted positions which he held in the service of the various courts. All previous commentators had been too far removed from worldly events to enable them to possess a proper evaluation and estimate of the historical and social background of Scripture. Abravanel, who had himself taken a prominent part in the politics of the day, perceived that the political and social life of the people had to be taken into consideration, and he estimates with considerable accuracy the historical standpoint. He successfully reconstructs the social background, and skilfully applies his practical experience of statecraft to the elucidation of the historical books. This is a subject for a lecture in itself, and I will therefore content myself with one example, which may be of interest. The 4th chapter of I Kings gives us the list of Solomon's court, and I give in parallel passages the translation of the A.V. and Abravanel's exposition.

[1] *Comm. on Samuel*, Introd.

A.V.	Abravanel
And these were the princes which he had; Azariah b. Zadok the priest, Elihoreph and Ahijah the sons of Shisha, scribes; Jehoshaphat son of Ahilud the recorder. And Benaiah b. Jehoiada was over the host, and Zadok and Abiathar were the priests, and Azariah the son of Nathan was over the officers, and Zabud b. Nathan was principal officer and the king's friend. And Ahishar was over the household and Adoniram b. Abda was over the tribute.	And this was the Council of State which he had. Azariah b. Zadok the priest and Elihoreph and Ahijah the sons of Shisha were the three scribes, one the Lord Chancellor, one the Chancellor of the Exchequer, and one the king's Secretary. And Jehoshaphat son of Ahilud was Procurator-Fiscal (sic)[1] And Benaiah b. Jehoiada was Commander in Chief. And Zadok and Abiathar were High Priests, and Azariah b. Nathan was head of the Provincial Department, and Zabud b. Nathan was the King's boon companion. And Ahishar was major-domo (sic)[1] and Adoniram was Chief of Excise.

A word must be said about Abravanel's use of *Midrashim*, since he himself, in the above-mentioned passage from his Introduction to Joshua, makes mention of it. On the one hand he deplores Rashi's too close adherence to homiletical exposition, on the other hand he criticizes Ḳimḥi for his total disregard of *Midrashim*. Abravanel deftly steers a middle course between these two extremes. He never allows the homiletical exposition of the Rabbis to influence his own commentary, but he takes every opportunity, even at the expense of sometimes far-fetched interpretations of the *Midrashim*, of showing how his exposition agrees with the interpretation of the passage in question by the ancient Rabbis. As a result his commentary, while retaining its rational and original character (see Addenda, p. 92), is a very treasure house of the choicest pearls of rabbinic and midrashic lore.

Among the finest and most enduring things which Abravanel wrote are what I call his excursus, long and detailed notes,

[1] These are the actual words used, in Hebrew transliteration.

which are often found repeated almost word for word in other parts of his commentary, on subjects of interest which had hitherto been dealt with either not at all, or inadequately. In them he has the opportunity, of which he takes every advantage, of giving full play to his vast erudition. He deals in detail with such varied subjects, which crop up in the course of his commentary, as (1) the origin, development and different kinds of Hebrew poetry and its dependence upon Arabic models,[1] (2) the history and inner meaning of the Rite of Anointing,[2] (3) the Wisdom of Solomon compared with that of other sages,[3] (4) the distinction between Judges and Kings,[4] (5) the Ark,[5] (6) on sacrifices,[6] (7) on forbidden foods and ritual uncleanness,[7] (8) on monarchy,[8] (9) on the meaning of Edom in the Bible.[9]

Each one of these is replete with original research and the result of painstaking study, but a brief précis of the last will sufficiently illustrate both the profundity of his knowledge and his methods.

He commences by stating that it is a commonly accepted tradition by Jewish writers from the earliest times, that Edom in the Bible refers to Rome. Solomon Levi however, who embraced the dominant faith and became Archbishop Paul of Burgos, quotes Nicholas de Lyra, whom Abravanel calls "the great Christian exegete", as denying this identity, but, not content with this, his hatred of the faith in which he was born is so great that he goes further than Lyra, and even tries to prove that Edom in the Bible refers to the Jewish people!

Now, continues Abravanel, had Archbishop Paul been thorough in his methods, he could have adduced the following additional arguments to disprove the identity of Edom with Rome, and he solemnly proceeds to enumerate an exhaustive list of biblical passages not quoted by Lyra or Paul of Burgos which tend to show that Edom cannot be identified with Rome. Having made this *beau geste*, he now proceeds to his

---

[1] Exod. xv, 1, and Isa. III, 1.　　[2] I Kings I, 34, and Exod. xxx, 30.
[3] I Kings III, 12.　　[4] Introduction to Judges.
[5] I Sam. IV, 4.　　[6] Jer. VII, 22.
[7] Lev. XI, 13.　　[8] I Sam. VIII, 4; Deut. XVII, 14.
[9] Isa. xxxIV, 6.

main task of demolishing Paul of Burgos' arguments and of confirming the Jewish tradition, and it is in the difficult task of showing the racial connection between the original inhabitants of the land south-east of Palestine, and the Roman Empire that he presses his vast learning into service, quoting among others Isidore of Seville and his *Etymologarium*.

Migration of tribes was very common in ancient days, and according to Josephus, when Joseph and his brethren went up to bury their father, the dukes of Edom attacked them. Joseph defeated them and took Zepho, the grandson of Esau, captive to Egypt. Zepho and his men escaped and found refuge in Africa and Carthaginia, whence they came to Italy. Here they were received with enthusiasm and Zepho, being made king, changed his name to Janus, and this name is preserved in Genoa. He reigned for fifty years in Campania and was the first king of Italy. He gives one or two other "proofs" from Jewish literature, fortifies them by references to Roman literature, and assumes that the knowledge of an Edomite king in Italy brought thousands of Edomites from their native land to Italy, where they prospered and became the dominating element. An arithmetical computation shows that the traditional date of the arrival of Janus from the East, according to Roman literature, 1500 years before Christ, was six years after the death of Jacob.

Having disposed in this manner of the racial aspect of the question, he has now to deal with the religious, viz. the ascription of Edom to Christianity. He justifies this by an interesting statement of the spiritual brotherliness between Judaism and Christianity. "Both of them agree that we have all one father, the God of gods, the First Cause, to whom they turn, without recourse to idols or supermundane spirits. Both have one Torah, for both have accepted the law of Moses in truth." But Abravanel is a Jew, and he therefore continues, "Christianity serves God, as did Esau his father, with ideas which are not true, while Judaism is in possession of the true faith. Thirdly, as Esau pained his father by marrying strange wives, so the true faith of Christianity has suffered by a foreign admixture of paganism". So he goes on with his comparisons, and again quotes Nicholas de Lyra, "the great Christian Biblical exegete", that Esau represents the enemies of the Jews, and he suggests that the name Yeshua', Jesus, is but a transposition of the name Esau written *plene*. An exposition of a Midrash to fortify his argument follows, and concludes with an interesting theory of Naḥmanides, that it was among the Idumeans, whom John Hyrcanus forcibly converted to Judaism and whose uneasy attachment to that faith was well known, that the Apostles and other disciples of Jesus, when they fled from Jerusalem, found their first converts to the new faith, and from that time and for that reason the name Edom became synonymous with Christianity.

There is a double purpose underlying the commentary of Abravanel. He is sincerely anxious to reveal the rational meaning of Scripture, but, as he says in his Introduction to Joshua, the Bible is to him more than a secular book of history, and the revelation of the Divine intention is to him the real purpose of the scriptural record. To a certain extent, this idea runs through his whole commentary from the very earliest of his works, but the tendency becomes accentuated to an infinitely greater extent as a result of the catastrophe which befell the Jewish people, and in which he played such a prominent and personal part, the expulsion of the Jews from Spain. A more competent authority than myself is dealing with the Messianism of Abravanel, perhaps to him the most important aspect of his commentary, and I will therefore content myself with pointing out one thing which emerges with unmistakable clarity from a study of his commentary. In the works which he wrote in Spain there is no trace of Messianism, and his commentary is on the whole scientific and purely objective. As he states clearly, however, in his *Ma'yene hay-Yeshu'ah*, the expulsion of the Jews from Spain caused him to search desperately in the Divine Record for some solution to this inexplicable catastrophe. From this time onwards a marked change can be seen in his commentary. It now becomes subjective instead of objective, and we can see him feverishly and anxiously seeking for some message of consolation, some divine ray of light in the surrounding darkness. When all is dark around he projects himself into some rosy future of the imagination, and to such an extent does this passion grow upon him, that despite his intense application to the task of writing his commentaries he abruptly breaks off in the middle of his commentary on Isaiah to compose his three main Messianic works. In his Introduction to the *Ma'yene hay-Yeshu'ah* he says, "I said to myself, it is time to act for the Lord, to strengthen the hands of the feeble and the feet that stumble, to strengthen and console those ensnared in the Exile...to seek in the Book of the Lord for His good word...and to find therefrom an end of these wonders", and from this time onwards this becomes the main and almost conscious aim of his work.

As to how imminent he regarded the Advent can be seen in his remark[1] that the Messiah had already been born, in his seeing in the spread of the "French plague" (venereal disease) the beginning of the end, and in his definite state-ment[2] that the Messiah would come seven years from the time of his writing, i.e. 1502–3. As that date drew near, his faith did not waver. In his commentary on Zechariah[3] written in that year, he says, in reference to the coming of the Messiah, "That is, this year", and it may be that it was his disillusionment, and perhaps the fear of being scoffed at, that caused him in the same year to leave Naples for Venice. But it did not deter him in his speculations. He merely made another numerical juggle and maintained that the former year was but the beginning, but the true Advent would be in 1534[4] or 1542.[5] The Christians will fight against the Arabs for possession of Palestine, which will then be granted to the Jews.[6]

More or less connected with his Messianism are his views on certain subjects, with a brief review of which I shall bring this lecture to an end. They are (1) Christianity, (2) monar-chy, (3) the Second Temple, (4) the settlement of the Jews in Europe.

---

[1] *M.Y.* xii, 7.
[3] Ezek. xx (f. 183*d*).
[5] Isa. xxxiv, 1 (f. 53*b*).

[2] Zech. xiv, 12; *M.Y.* xi, x.
[4] *M.Y.* xii, 2.
[6] Jer. xxx, 2 (f. 129*b*).

(1) *Christianity.* Throughout the whole of his commentary Abravanel sets out consciously and deliberately to controvert the Christological exposition of the Bible. On points unrelated to theology, he readily accepts the views of Christian scholars, sometimes in preference to those of Jewish authorities;[1] in points of doctrine he is merciless in his opposition to their views. His knowledge both of the history and the theology of Christianity was profound and extensive. He deals[2] with a wealth of detail with the life of Jesus, the conversion of Constantine to Christianity, the Crusades, and the conquest of Palestine with the reconquest by the Saracens. He had read the Vulgate and the New Testament and the work of every Christian theologian of note.[3] His description[4] of the Papal hierarchy and the election of Cardinals is interesting and accurate. His treatment of the subject is often fair and extensive, for instance, his proof[5] that the "root of Jesse" cannot refer to Jesus, but as often as not it is to be regretted that he contents himself, after stating the Christian view, with the terse question[6] "What need is there for me to refute such triflings?"

Nevertheless, there is little trace of bitterness, nor too pronounced a bias, but so lucid and sometimes devastating is his *exposé*, that it is not to be wondered at that, despite the popularity of his works among Christian scholars, his commentary on Isaiah was forbidden by the Popes to be studied.[7]

(2) *Monarchy.* Abravanel is probably the sole rabbinical commentator to be a profound and sincere Republican. There is generally in Judaism a strong monarchical tradition, and no commentator before him or after has cast doubt upon the divinity of the institution of monarchy. But Abravanel's experience at the courts of kings, his profound knowledge of Roman history which showed him that the Golden Age of Roman history was the period when it was ruled by consuls, his deep admiration of the republics of Venice, Florence, Genoa, etc., all tended to make him doubt the value of

---

[1] I Kings v (f. 216*d fin.*, f. 222*d fin.*), I Sam. III, 4.   [2] Isa. IX, 5 (f. 23*a seq.*).
[3] Cf. *Comm. on Joshua*, Introd.   [4] Isa. XXV, 2.   [5] Isa. X, 1.
[6] Isa. IX, 5 (f. 23*a fin.*).
[7] E. H. Lindo, Bibliographical notes to the *Conciliator*.

monarchy.[1] Not only has he two long excursus[2] on it, but he takes every opportunity of expressing the superiority of republics over monarchies. In Messianic times there were to be no kings or princes, since all would be equal.[3] The remarkable thing is that he wrote both these passages while he was still under a monarchical system, and actually in the service of the king, and it is noteworthy in this connection that despite the devastating effect which the expulsion of the Jews from Spain had upon him, his description of Ferdinand in his Introduction to the *Ma'yene hay-Yeshu'ah* is a most sympathetic one. Isabella he passes over almost in silence.

(3) *The Second Temple.* One of his most peculiar views is his constantly repeated assertion[4] that the return of the Jews to Palestine subsequent to the Proclamation of Cyrus was not the Redemption heralded by the Prophets, nor was the Second Temple a real temple. It is just as though, he says, the Arab ruler of Jerusalem of his day had granted permission to all the Jews in other parts of his dominion to settle in that part of his dominion which is Palestine. So Cyrus permitted his Babylonian Jewish subjects to settle in Palestine, but it did not affect the Jews scattered throughout the world. His underlying purpose is obvious. It was in order to prove that the glorious prophecies of the Redemption by the pre-exilic prophets had not yet been fulfilled. Their fulfilment was still a promise of the future, and thus there was still hope for his afflicted brethren.

(4) *The settlement of the Jews in Europe.* It is obvious from this that Abravanel was of the opinion that the Jews were exiled beyond Babylon as a result of the First Exile, and indeed he maintains, time and again, that the settlement of the Jews in Europe dates from the Exile of Nebuchadnezzar. Moses ibn Ezra was probably the first to state this with regard to Spain,[5] but Abravanel not only gives full details, but extends the Exile to France and England.

---

[1] Sam. VIII, 4; Deut. XVII, 14.
[2] Judges VIII, 7 (f. 66b), I Sam. X, 17 (f. 98c and d).
[3] End of § 12 of *Comm. on Isaiah.*
[4] Jer. XXXII, 1; XXVII, XXX. Lev. XXVI, 28; end of II Kings; Deut. XXVIII, 15; Isa. XIV, 1; XIX, 1.   [5] *J.E.* VI, 525; *R.E.J.* XXI, XXII.

This is a convenient place to make mention of one pecu-
liarity of Abravanel which I have made the subject of a paper
read before the Jewish Historical Society of England. Not
only does Abravanel show an intimate knowledge of English
customs, history and legend, but he appears to take every
opportunity of making allusions to "Inglaterra", even where
the text he is explaining, or the example he is adducing, does
not justify it, and in nearly every case the insertion of the
word "Inglaterra" makes an otherwise correct statement
erroneous. This predilection for inserting references to England
I have ascribed to the fact that for close upon a quarter of a
century Abravanel was in the service of the King of Portugal,
England's oldest ally, strongly linked to it by economic
interests, by intermarriage between the respective royal
houses, and by military expeditions sent from England to
Portugal. He was thus in a position to glean information
concerning this country.

Thus, like other commentators on Obad. I, 20, he equates
Zarapath with France and Sepharad with Spain, but he adds
England to these; he includes English soldiers with the
armies of Titus (Deut. xxviii, 49) and the First Crusade
(*M.Y.* II, 3); he mentions England with France and Germany
as producing wine (Isa. v, 1). He states that "Isle de
France" was the ancient name of England (*Mash. Y.* ix, 1);
that St Helena was deemed a British princess (*M.Y.* to
Dan. II, 17); he knew John de Mandeville (Ezek. Introd.)
and the Venerable Bede (*M.Y.* x, 7 and viii), and also about
sheep-rearing in England (Exod. xxiii, 19) and pre-Expulsion
Anglo-Jewish history (Isa. xliii, 5).

Abravanel is a Fundamentalist of Fundamentalists. Every
word of the Bible is to him of direct divine origin. In his
explanation of the discrepancies and contradictions between
parallel texts he vigorously repudiates the theory adduced by
Ibn Ezra that one is a paraphrase, in the author's own words,
of the divine statement of the other, and perhaps the best
example of his naïve faith is his discussion how Jochebed
could be the mother of Moses.· He explains that an old man
can have children by a young wife, and then says, "But

what need is there for me to bring examples of this possibility from history, since the Bible itself gives us such examples?"[1]

Some of his exegesis can, without exaggeration, be termed not only original but brilliant. He stands alone, without predecessor and without follower. The last of the great Spanish school of exegetes, his original method gives him a just claim to a position of splendid isolation; the rapid decline of rational exposition among Jews prevented him from having followers. A host of Christian scholars from the sixteenth to eighteenth centuries used his work and translated it, but to-day one may state without contradiction that he is too much underrated and neglected.

In a book recently published,[2] there is included a reprint of Book III of Isaac Da Costa's *Israel and the Gentiles*, in which the author makes the following astonishing statement in the course of a brief account of Abravanel: "His proud and ambitious spirit led him to seek by preference the worldly duties of a politician, while he gave free vent to his inveterate hatred against the persecutors of his people, and, alas! against the Christian religion....In viewing Abravanel's character as a whole, we must class him rather among the brilliant intellects than the noble characters of the dispersed of Israel."

This was originally written in 1850, and the editor of the book to which I refer says in his Preface, "Statements made by Da Costa nearly 100 years ago may naturally often require some modification and correction in view of modern research."

Of the statement quoted the least that can be said is that neither modification nor correction will meet the case. A more unfair statement of Abravanel's works and character it would be hard to find. Of criticism of Christianity there is naturally much; of hatred, none. Brilliant his intellect may have been; but it pales into insignificance before the nobility of character, the steadfastness of his faith, the generous appreciation of the virtues of Christianity and even of his persecutors which emerges from a study of his work, and to which I have made brief reference.

[1] On Exod. II, 1. [2] *Noble families among the Sephardic Jews*, p. 70, Oxford, 1936.

There is a beautiful Midrash which describes the immortality of the spirit by saying that when one repeats the words of a dead master, his lips move in the grave, and if this celebration of the quingentenary of Abravanel will bring about what will undoubtedly be a profitable study of his work, the immortality of Don Isaac b. Judah Abravanel, statesman and scholar, will be assured.

ADDENDA

P. 79. Of the many examples which could be quoted, the two following are of more than passing interest:

(a) His description of the Bene-Israel in India, culled from a letter brought by Portuguese spice merchants from India (Jer. III, 16, f. 102 b; *Mashmia' Yeshu'ah*, III, 3).

(b) His statement that doctors can determine the sex of an unborn child by examining the urine of a pregnant woman (Isa. VII, 14, f. 20 a).

P. 83. The following examples of original and rational exegesis of Abravanel may be quoted:

(a) In Exod. I, 15 for Hebrew "midwives" (R.V.) he has "The (Egyptian) midwives for the Hebrew Women". For, he pertinently asks, would Pharaoh have been so foolish as to appoint Hebrew women for this heartless task?

(b) Exod. II, 10. He translates this verse: "And she (Moses' mother) called his name Moses, saying (to Pharaoh's daughter), Because *thou didst draw him* from the water."

(c) Josh. II, 1. On the Targum rendering of *Zonah* (lit. harlot) as an innkeeper, Abravanel makes the point that the Targum does not deny that she was a harlot, but merely wishes to explain that innkeeping was the cloak under which she carried on her immoral calling. He then translates verse 4 as an admission by Rahab of her profession, on the analogy of Gen. XXIX, 21.

Lecture V

ON ABRAVANEL'S PHILOSOPHICAL
TENDENCY AND POLITICAL
TEACHING

BY DR L. STRAUSS

ON ABRAVANEL'S PHILOSOPHICAL TENDENCY AND POLITICAL TEACHING[1]

ABRAVANEL may be called the last of the Jewish philosophers of the Middle Ages. He belongs to the Middle Ages, as far as the framework and the main content of his doctrine are concerned. It is true that there are features of his thought which distinguish it from that of all or of most other Jewish medieval philosophers; but most of those features are probably of medieval Christian origin. Yet Abravanel is a son of the humanist age, and thus we shall not be surprised if he expresses in his writings opinions or tendencies which are, to say the least, not characteristic of the Middle Ages. Generally speaking, however, Abravanel is a medieval thinker, a Jewish medieval thinker.

The central figure in the history of Jewish medieval philosophy is Maimonides. Thus it will be advisable to define the character of Abravanel's philosophical tendency by contrasting it with that of Maimonides. One is all the more justified in proceeding thus, since there is scarcely any other philosopher whom Abravanel admired so much, or whom he followed as much, as he did Maimonides.

What was then the general tendency of Maimonides? The answer to this question seems to be obvious: Maimonides attempted to harmonize the teachings of Jewish tradition with the teachings of philosophical tradition, i.e. of the Aristotelian tradition. This answer is certainly not altogether wrong, but it is quite insufficient, since it fails to explain which ultimate assumptions enabled Maimonides to harmonize Judaism and Aristotle. Now those truly decisive assumptions are neither of Jewish nor of Aristotelian origin: they are borrowed from Plato, from Plato's political philosophy.

At a first glance, the philosophical tradition from which

[1] I wish to express my thanks to the Board of the Faculty of History for a grant enabling this essay to be written and to Mrs M. C. Blackman for kindly revising the English.

Maimonides starts seems to be identical with that which is the determining factor of Christian scholasticism. Indeed, to Maimonides as well as to Thomas Aquinas, Aristotle is *the* philosopher. There is, however, one striking and at the same time highly important difference between Maimonides and the Christian scholastic as regards the philosophical tradition on which they build. For Thomas Aquinas, Aristotle is the highest authority, not only in other branches of philosophy, but also in political philosophy. Maimonides, on the other hand, could not use Aristotle's *Politics*, since it had not been translated into Arabic or Hebrew; but he could start, and he did start, from Plato's political philosophy.[1] For the *Republic* and the *Laws*, which were inaccessible to the Latin Middle Ages,[2] had been translated into Arabic in the ninth century, and commentaries on them had been written by two of the most outstanding Islamic philosophers.[3] By considering these facts we gain, I believe, a clear impression of the philosophical difference which exists between the philosophy of Maimonides (and of his Islamic predecessors) on the one hand, and that of Christian scholasticism on the other: the place occupied in the latter by Aristotle's *Politics* is occupied in the former by Plato's *Republic* and *Laws*. I have read that in some Italian pictures Plato is represented holding in his hand the *Timaeus* and Aristotle his *Ethics*. If a pupil of Maimonides or of the Islamic philosophers[4] had found pleasure in representations

---

[1] For details I must refer the reader for the time being to my book *Philosophie und Gesetz*, Berlin (Schocken), 1935, and to my article "Quelques remarques sur la science politique de Maimonide et de Farabi", *Revue des Études Juives*, 1936, pp. 1–37.

[2] Cp. Ernest Barker, *Plato and his Predecessors*, p. 383: "For a thousand years the *Republic* has no history; for a thousand years it simply disappeared. From the days of Proclus, the Neo-Platonist of the fifth century, almost until the days of Marsilio Ficino and Pico della Mirandola, at the end of the fifteenth, the *Republic* was practically a lost book." The same holds true, as far as the Latin Middle Ages are concerned, of the *Laws*.

[3] Farabi's paraphrase of the *Laws* will be edited in the near future by Dr Paul Kraus. The original of Averroes' paraphrase of the *Republic* seems to be lost; but this paraphrase is accessible in an often-printed Latin translation. The more reliable Hebrew translation is being edited by Dr Erwin Rosenthal; see *Journ. Roy. Asiatic Soc.*, October 1934, pp. 737 ff.

[4] When speaking of Islamic philosophers, I am limiting myself strictly to the *falāsifa*, the so-called Aristotelians.

of this kind, he might have chosen rather the inverse order: Aristotle with his *Physics* or *Metaphysics* and Plato with his *Republic* or *Laws*.

For what is the meaning of the fact that Maimonides and the Islamic philosophers whom he followed start from Platonic political philosophy, and not from Aristotle's *Politics*? One cannot avoid raising this question, especially since the circumstance that the *Politics* was not translated into Arabic may well be, not a mere matter of chance, but the result of a deliberate choice, made in the beginning of this medieval development. Now, in order to answer that question, we must remind ourselves of the general character of the medieval world, and of the particular character of the Islamic philosophy adopted by Maimonides. The medieval world is distinguished both from the classical and from the modern world by the fact that its thought was fundamentally determined by the belief in Revelation. Revelation was the determining factor with the Islamic philosophers as well as with the Jewish and Christian philosophers. But, as was clearly recognized by such contemporary and competent observers as Ghazzâli, Maimonides and Thomas Aquinas, the Islamic philosophers did not believe in Revelation properly speaking. They were philosophers in the classical sense of the word: men who would hearken to reason, and to reason only. Consequently, they were compelled to give an account of the Revelation which they had to accept and which they did accept, in terms of human reason. Their task was facilitated by the fact that Revelation, as understood by Jews or Muslims, had the form of law. Revelation, thus understood, lent itself to being interpreted by loyal philosophers as a perfect, ideal law, as an ideal political order. Moreover, the Islamic philosophers were compelled, and so was Maimonides, to justify their pursuit of philosophy before the law to which they were subject; they had, therefore, to prove that the law did not only entitle them, but even oblige them, to devote themselves to philosophy. Consequently, they were driven to interpret Revelation more precisely as an ideal political order, the ideal character of which consists in the very fact that it lays upon all men endowed with the necessary qualities the duty of devoting their lives to philosophy, that it awakens them to philosophy, that it holds out for their guidance at least the most important tenets of philosophy. For this purpose they had to assume that the founder of the ideal political order, the prophetic lawgiver, was not merely a statesman, but that he was, at the same time, a philosopher of the highest authority: they had to conceive, and they did conceive, of Moses or Mohammed as philosopher kings. Philosopher kings and a political community governed by philosopher kings were, however, the theme, not of Aristotelian but of Platonic political philosophy. Thus we may say: Maimonides and his Islamic predecessors start from Platonic political philosophy, because they had to conceive of the Revelation to which they were subject, as of an ideal political order, the specific purpose of which was guidance to philosophy. And we may add that their belief in the authority of Moses or Mohammed was perhaps not greatly different from what would have been the belief of a later Greek Platonist in the authority of Plato, if that Platonist had been the citizen of a commonwealth governed by Plato's *Laws*.

Judaism on the one hand, Aristotelianism on the other,. certainly supplied the greatest part of the matter of Maimonides' teaching. But Platonic political philosophy provided at any rate the framework for the two achievements by which Maimonides made an epoch in the history of Judaism: for his codification of the Jewish law and for his philosophical defence of the Jewish law. It is open to question which of Plato's political works was the most important for Maimonides and the Islamic philosophers. But it is safe to say that the best clue to the understanding of their teaching is supplied by the *Laws*.[1] I cannot discuss here the true meaning of this most ironical of Plato's works, although I believe that only

---

[1] E. Barker, *loc. cit.* p. 351, says with regard to the Latin Middle Ages: "The end of the *Laws* is the beginning of the Middle Ages." This statement is all the more true of the Islamic and Jewish Middle Ages. Compare, for example, the quotations from Avicenna in *Philosophie und Gesetz*, p. 111, and from R. Sheshet in *Revue des Études Juives*, 1936, p. 2, n. 1.

the full understanding of its true meaning would enable us to understand adequately the medieval philosophy of which I am speaking. For our present purpose, it is sufficient to state that the *Laws* are certainly the primary source of the opinions which Maimonides and his teachers held concerning the relation between philosophy and Revelation, or, more exactly, between philosophy and law. Those opinions may be summarized in the following ways: (1) Law is based on certain fundamental beliefs or dogmas of a strictly philosophical character, and those beliefs are, as it were, the prelude to the whole law. The beliefs of this kind were called by Fârâbî, who was, according to Maimonides, the highest philosophical authority of his period, "opinions of the people of the excellent city". (2) Law contains, apart from those rational beliefs, a number of other beliefs which, while being not properly true, but representing the truth in a disguised way, are necessary or useful in the interest of the political community. The beliefs of this type may be called, as they were by Spinoza, who was, perhaps, the latest exponent of that medieval tradition, *pia dogmata*, in contradistinction to the *vera dogmata* of the first group.[1] (3) Necessary beliefs, i.e. the beliefs which are not common to philosophy and law, but peculiar to law as such, are to be defended (either by themselves or together with the whole law) by probable, persuasive, rhetorical arguments, not recognizable as such to the vulgar; a special science is to be devoted to that "defence of the law" or "assistance to the law".

We are now in a position to define more precisely the character of Maimonides' attempt to harmonize the Jewish tradition with the philosophical tradition. He effects the harmony between those two traditions by starting from the conception of a perfect law, perfect in the sense of Plato's *Laws*, i.e. of a law leading to the study of philosophy and based on philosophical truth, and by thus proving that Judaism is a law of this character. To prove this, he shows that the fundamental beliefs of Judaism are identical with the fundamental tenets of philosophy, i.e. with those tenets

---

[1] *Tractatus theologico-politicus*, ch. 14 (§20, Bruder).

on which an ideal law ought to be based. By showing this, he shows, at the same time, that those Jewish beliefs which are of an unphilosophical nature are meant by the Jewish legislator himself, by *the* philosopher legislator, to be necessary beliefs, i.e. beliefs necessary for political reasons. The assumption underlying this proof of the ideal character of the Jewish law is the opinion that the law has two different meanings: an exterior, literal meaning, addressed to the vulgar, which expresses both the philosophical and the necessary beliefs, and a secret meaning of a purely philosophical nature. Now this property of law had to be imitated by Maimonides in his philosophic interpretation of the law. For if he had distinguished explicitly between true and necessary beliefs, he would have endangered the acceptance of the necessary beliefs on which the authority of the law with the vulgar, i.e. with the great majority, rests. Consequently, he could make this essential distinction only in a disguised way, partly by allusions, partly by the composition of his whole work, but mainly by the rhetorical character, recognizable only to philosophers, of the arguments by which he defends the necessary beliefs. As a consequence, Maimonides' philosophical work, the *Guide of the Perplexed*, is a most ingenious combination of "opinions of the people of the excellent city", i.e. of a strictly demonstrative discussion of the beliefs which are common to philosophy and law, with "defence of the law", i.e. with a rhetorical discussion of the unphilosophical beliefs peculiar to the law. Thus not only the law itself, but also Maimonides' philosophical interpretation of the law, has two different meanings: a literal meaning, addressed to the more unphilosophic reader of philosophic education, which is very near to the traditional Jewish beliefs, and a secret meaning, addressed to true philosophers, which is purely philosophical. This amounts to saying that Maimonides' philosophical work was liable to, and was intended to be liable to, two fundamentally different interpretations: to a "radical" interpretation which did honour to the consistency of his thought, and to a "moderate" interpretation which did honour rather to the fervour of his belief.

The ambiguous nature of Maimonides' philosophical work must be recognized if one wants to judge properly of the general tendency of Abravanel. For Abravanel has to be characterized, to begin with, as a strict, even passionate adherent of the literal interpretation of the *Guide of the Perplexed*. The more philosophic interpretation of this work had appealed to some earlier commentators. Those commentators, who were under the spell of Islamic philosophy rather than of Christian scholasticism, are vehemently attacked by Abravanel,[1] who finds words of the highest praise for the Christian scholastics.[2] But Abravanel accepts the literal teaching of the *Guide* not only as the true expression of Maimonides' thought: that literal teaching is at the same time, if not identical with, at least the framework of, Abravanel's own philosophy.

The beliefs peculiar to the law are founded upon and, as it were, derived from one fundamental conviction: the belief in *creatio ex nihilo*.[3] That belief had been defended by Maimonides in his *Guide* with great care and vigour. The discussion of the creation of the world, or, in other words, the criticism of the contention of the philosophers that the visible world is eternal, forms literally the central part of the *Guide*. It is the central part of this work also because of the fact that the interpretation of the whole work depends on the interpretation of this very part. Indeed, this is the crucial question for the interpretation of Maimonides' philosophical work: whether the discussion of the question of creation expresses Maimonides' own opinion in a direct way, or whether it is in the service of the "defence of the law". However one may answer this question, the very question itself implies the recognition of the fact that the literal teaching of the *Guide* is most decidedly in favour of the belief in creation. Now

---

[1] Cp. his judgements on Ibn Kaspi and others, quoted by Jacob Guttmann, *Die religionsphilosophischen Lehren des Isaak Abravanel*, Breslau, 1916, pp. 34–6 and 71.

[2] See his commentary on Josh. x, 12 (f. 21, col. 2). I have used Abravanel's commentary on Joshua, Judges, Samuel and Kings in the Frankfort edition of 1736.

[3] Cp. Abravanel, *Rosh 'Amanah*, ch. 22, with Maimonides' *Guide*, Pt. II, ch. 25 in the beginning, and Pt. III, ch. 25 in the end.

while Maimonides carefully maintains this belief, on which all other beliefs peculiar to the law depend, he takes a rather hesitating, if not self-contradictory position, as regards those other beliefs, i.e. as regards belief in the miracles, in Revelation, in the immortality of the soul, in individual providence, in resurrection. If he actually believed in *creatio ex nihilo*, he was as little under a stringent necessity to depreciate those beliefs, or to restrict their bearing, as were the Christian scholastics, who also had combined Aristotelianism with the belief in creation, and who accepted the Christian dogma as a whole. Abravanel accepted Maimonides' explicit doctrine of the creation as true—he defended it in a special treatise (*Shamayim Hadashim*), and he knew Christian scholasticism. It was, therefore, only natural that he should have defended, and that he did defend, on the very basis of Maimonides' doctrine of creation and against his authority, all the other beliefs which are dependent on the belief in creation and which Maimonides had endangered. Thus, his criticism of Maimonides' dangerous doctrines is, in principle, not more than an immanent criticism of the literal teaching of the *Guide*; it is not more than a subsequent correction of that teaching in the sense of the Jewish traditional beliefs. It would not be much of an exaggeration to say that Abravanel's philosophical exertions as a whole are a defence of the Jewish creed, as drawn up by Maimonides in his commentary to the Mishnah, against the implications, dangerous to this creed, of the teaching of the *Guide*.

The creed compiled by Maimonides was defended expressly by Abravanel in a special treatise (*Rosh 'Amanah*). This treatise, by itself perhaps the most striking evidence of the admiration which Abravanel felt for Maimonides, gives us a clear idea both of Abravanel's own tendency and of his interpretation of Maimonides. Maimonides' arrangement of the Jewish beliefs, the so-called "Thirteen Articles of Faith", had been attacked by some later Jewish writers for philosophical as well as for religious reasons. Abravanel defends Maimonides against those critics by showing that Jewish orthodoxy is perfectly defined by the recognition of just those thirteen articles which Maimonides had selected, and that the order of those articles is completely lucid. As regards the latter point, Abravanel asserts that the former part of those articles indicates the beliefs common to philosophy and law, while the latter part is concerned with those beliefs which either are not accepted, or which are even contested by the philosophers.[1] It is not necessary for our purpose to dwell on the detail of Abravanel's arguments. One point only must be stressed. After having devoted twenty-two chapters to defending Maimonides' compilation, Abravanel rather abruptly explains, in the two concluding chapters of his treatise, that a creed as such is incompatible with the character of Judaism as a divinely given law. For since any and every proposition of the law, any and every story, belief, or command contained in the law, immediately proceeds from Revelation, all those propositions are of equal value, and none of them ought to be thought of as more fundamental than any other. Abravanel does not think that by holding this opinion he is in conflict with the teaching of Maimonides; strangely enough, he asserts that that opinion was shared by Maimonides himself. According to Abravanel, Maimonides selected the thirteen more general articles of belief for the use of the vulgar only, who are unable to grasp the whole doctrine of faith. To prove this statement, he contends that Maimonides mentioned those articles only in his commentary to the Mishnah, i.e. in an elementary work which he wrote in his youth, but not in the Guide, in which he treats the philosophy of the Jewish law in a scientific way. Now this contention is not only wrong, but it is contradicted by Abravanel himself. He asserts, in the same treatise,[2] that the articles of belief—the first eleven out of the thirteen explicitly, the last two implicitly—occur as such in the philosophical first part of Maimonides' codification of the Jewish law (in the Hilkhoth Yesodhe hat-Torah); and in another writing of his,[3] he explains the decisive influence exercised by the articles of belief on the whole composition of the Guide. But however this may be, it is certain that Abravanel, by

---

[1] Rosh 'Amanah, ch. 10. [2] Ch. 19.
[3] Ma'amar Qāṣēr bᵉBhi'ur Šōdh ham-Moreh.

denying the possibility of distinguishing between fundamental and non-fundamental beliefs, actually undermines the whole structure of the philosophy of the Jewish law which was built up by Maimonides.[1] Abravanel has sometimes been blamed for the inconsistency of his thought. I cannot praise him as a very consistent thinker. But a certain consistency ought not to be denied him. Accepting the literal teaching of Maimonides' *Guide* and trying to correct that teaching in the sense of the traditional Jewish beliefs, he was consistent enough to draw the final conclusion from his premises: he contested, if only occasionally, the foundation on which every philosophy of the law divine ultimately rests. However deeply he may have been influenced by the philosophical tradition in general and by the philosophical teaching of Maimonides in particular, his thought was decisively determined, not by philosophy, but by Judaism as a tradition based on a verbally inspired revelation.

The unphilosophic, to some extent even anti-philosophic, traditionalism of Abravanel accounts for the fact that for him political philosophy loses the central importance which it had for Maimonides. From what has been said about Maimonides' philosophy of Judaism, it will have appeared that the significance which he actually attaches to political philosophy is in exact proportion to his rationalism: identifying the fundamental beliefs of Judaism with the fundamental tenets of philosophy means at the same time interpreting the beliefs peculiar to Judaism in terms of political philosophy; and it means, in principle, interpreting Judaism as a whole as a perfect law in the Platonic sense. Accordingly, a follower of Maimonides, who rejected the thoroughgoing rationalism of the latter, as did Abravanel, deprived by this very fact political philosophy of all its dignity. One cannot raise the objection against this assertion that the Christian scholastics,

---

[1] Cp. in this connection, Abravanel's criticism of Maimonides' explanation of the Mosaic laws; see his commentary on I Kings III, 14 (f. 210, col. 2) and his commentary on Deut. XII, 28 (f. 286, col. 4). (I have used Abravanel's commentary on the Pentateuch in the Hanau edition of 1710.) Cp. also his criticism of Gersonides' method of drawing maxims out of the biblical narratives in the introduction to the commentary on Joshua (f. 5, col. 2).

while far from being radical rationalists, did indeed cultivate political philosophy. For the case of those scholastics who were citizens of existing states was obviously quite different from the case of the Jewish medieval thinkers. For a medieval Jew, political philosophy could have no other field of application than the Jewish law. Consequently, the value which political philosophy could have for him was entirely dependent on how far he would accept philosophy in general and political philosophy in particular as a clue to the understanding of the Jewish law. Now according to Maimonides, the prophet, who brought the law, is a philosopher statesman, and at least the greater part of the Mosaic law is concerned with the "government of the city".[1] Abravanel, on the other hand, denies that philosophy in general is of the essence of prophecy. As regards political philosophy in particular, he declares that the prophet does not stoop to such "low" things as politics and economics. He stresses in this connection the fact that the originator of the biblical organization of jurisdiction was not Moses, but Jethro.[2] In making these statements, Abravanel does not contest that Moses, as well as the other prophets, exercised a kind of government. As we shall see later, he even asserts this expressly. But he obviously does not accept the view, presupposed by Maimonides, that prophetic government is a legitimate subject of political philosophy. Political philosophy, as he understands it, has a much more restricted field than it had for Maimonides; it is much more of the Aristotelian than of the Platonic type.[3] Abravanel's depreciation of political philosophy, which is a consequence of his critical attitude towards Maimonides' rationalism, thus implies a decisive limitation of the content of political philosophy.

Political philosophy, as outlined by Maimonides, had dealt with three main topics: the prophet, the king and the

---

[1] *Guide*, Pt. III, ch. 27–28.

[2] Commentary on I Kings III, 14 (f. 211, col. 1). Cp. however the commentary on Exod. XVIII, 13–27 (f. 134, col. 2–3).

[3] As regards Abravanel's knowledge of Aristotle's *Politics*, see J. F. Baer, "Don Jizchaq Abravanel", *Tarbiz*, VIII, pp. 241 f., 245 n. 11 and 248. See also below, p. 113, n. 2. In his commentary on Gen. X, 1 ff. (f. 40, col. 1) Abravanel seems occasionally to adopt the Aristotelian doctrine of natural masters and servants.

Messiah. According to Maimonides, the prophet as such is a philosopher statesman, and the highest prophet, Moses, was that philosopher statesman who was able to give the perfect, and consequently eternal, unchangeable law.[1] As regards kingship, Maimonides teaches that the institution of a king is indispensable, and expressly commanded by the Mosaic law. The king is subordinate to the lawgiver; his function is to force men to obedience to the law, to establish justice and to be the military leader. He himself is bound by the law and, therefore, subject both to punishment in case of transgression of the law and to instruction by the supreme court, the guardians of the law. The king has extraordinary powers in case of urgent necessity, and his claims both to honour and to glory are acknowledged by the law.[2] The Messiah, as Maimonides conceives of him, is, in the first instance, a king, obedient to the law, and a successful military leader, who will rescue Israel from servitude, restore the kingdom of David in the country of Israel, establish universal peace, and thus create, for the first time in history, the ideal earthly condition for a life devoted to knowledge. But the Messiah is not only a king; he is, at the same time, a prophet of a rank not much inferior to that of the lawgiver Moses: the Messiah, too, is a philosopher king. Even according to the literal teaching of Maimonides, the Messiah does not work miracles, and the Messianic age in general does not witness any alteration of the ordinary course of nature. It goes almost without saying that that age is not the prelude to the end of the visible world: the present world will remain in existence for ever.[3] Thus we may define the distinctive features of Maimonides' Messianology by saying that Messianism, as he accepts it, is a rational hope rather than a superrational belief.[4] Maimonides' rationalism accounts in

---

[1] Cp. *Guide*, Pt. i, ch. 54 with Pt. ii, ch. 39–40.
[2] See *Guide*, Pt. ii, ch. 40; Pt. iii, ch. 41 (Munk, p. 91 *a*) and ch. 45 (Munk, p. 98 *b*) as well as *Hilkhoth Melakhim*, ch. 1, §§3 and 8; ch. 3 *passim*; ch. 4, §10 and ch. 5, §2.
[3] *Hilkhoth Melakhim*, ch. 11–12; *Hilkhoth Teshubah*, ch. 9; *Guide*, Pt. ii, ch. 29.
[4] Notice the distinction between "belief" and "hope" in *Hilkhoth Melakhim*, ch. 11, §1.

particular for the fact that he stresses so strongly the character of the Messiah as a successful military leader—he does this most definitely by inserting his thematic treatment of Messianology within that section of his great legal work which deals with "the kings and their wars". For military ability or deficiency seems to be the decisive natural reason for the rise or decline of states. Maimonides, at any rate, thinks that the reason for the destruction of the Jewish state in the past was the neglect of the arts of war and conquest.[1] Accordingly, he expects that military virtue and military ability will play a decisive part in the future restoration of the Jewish state.[2]

It is a necessary consequence of Abravanel's anti-rationalist premises that he must exclude the two most exalted topics of Maimonides' political philosophy from the field of political philosophy, properly speaking, altogether. As regards the prophets, the prophetic lawgiver and the law divine, he takes away their treatment from political philosophy by contesting the assertions of Maimonides that prophecy is a natural phenomenon,[3] and that philosophy belongs to the essence of prophecy.[4] For, by denying this, he destroys the foundation of Maimonides' conception of the prophet as a philosopher statesman. The leadership of the prophet, as Abravanel sees it, is, just as prophecy itself is, of an essentially supernatural, and thus of an essentially superpolitical character. As regards the Messiah, Abravanel devoted to this theme a much more detailed and a much more passionate treatment than Maimonides had done.[5] Indeed, as we are informed by a

[1] See his letter to the community at Marseilles.

[2] I am not competent to judge whether Maimonides' legal treatment of kings and wars is influenced by the Islamic conception of the Holy War. But it is certain that his stressing the importance of military virtue in his philosophic prophetology was influenced by the prophetology of the Islamic philosophers, who attach a much higher value to war and to the virtue of courage than Plato and Aristotle had done. Cp. *Revue des Études Juives*, 1936, pp. 19 f. and 35 f.

[3] See Abravanel's commentary on *Guide*, Pt. II, ch. 32.

[4] See, for example, commentary on I Kings III, 14 (f. 210, col. 4).

[5] In this connection, the fact has to be mentioned that some prophecies which, according to Maimonides, were fulfilled in the past, i.e. at a time comparatively near to their announcement, are interpreted by Abravanel as Messianic prophecies. Cp. the interpretation given in *Guide*, Pt. II, ch. 29, of Isa. XXIV, 17 ff. and Joel III, 3–5, with Abravanel's explanations of those passages in his commentary on the later prophets.

most competent historian, Abravanel stressed in his writings
the Messianic hopes more than any other Jewish medieval
author, and he was the first to give the Messianic beliefs of
Israel a systematic form.[1] This increase of the interest in
eschatological speculation is explained by the fact that
Abravanel was a contemporary of the greatest revolutions in
the history of the Jewish diaspora, and of that great revolution of European civilization which is called the end of the
Middle Ages and the beginning of the modern period.
Abravanel expected the coming of the Messiah in the near
future. He saw signs of its imminence in all the characteristic
features of his time, from the increase of heresies and unbelief
down to the appearance of the "French disease".[2] Reflections
of this kind show that his Messianistic view was not, as was,
at least to some extent, that of Maimonides, of an evolutionist,
but of a catastrophic character. It is hardly necessary to add
that the Messianic age is for Abravanel a period rich in
miracles, the most impressive of them being the resurrection
of the dead. That age, which is the age of universal peace, even
among the animals, as predicted by Isaiah, lasts only for a
limited time; it is followed by the end of the present world.[3]
It is preceded by a most terrible war, the final war. That war
is, however, not so much a war of liberation, fought and won
by Israel as Maimonides had taught; it is rather an event
like the capture of Jericho, as told in the book of Joshua:
Israel is a looker-on at the victory rather than the victor.[4]
Accordingly, in Abravanel's description of the Messiah,[5] the
military abilities and virtues are, to say the least, not pre-
dominant.[6] To him, the Messiah is certainly much more a

[1] Baer, *loc. cit.* pp. 257–9.
[2] That disease is, according to Abravanel, probably meant in Zech. xiv, 12
(see his commentary on that passage).
[3] See G. Scholem's remark in *Encyc. Judaica*, ix, col. 688.
[4] The "realistic" element of Abravanel's conception of the final war, i.e.
his identification of the final war with the war which he thought to be imminent
between the Christian nations of Europe and the Turks for Palestine, does not
change the character of his conception as a whole.
[5] See his commentary on Isa. xi.
[6] Those qualities, I venture to suggest, are ascribed by Abravanel not so
much to *the* Messiah (i.e. the Messiah ben David) as to the Messiah ben Joseph,
a Midrashic figure, not mentioned by Maimonides.

worker of miracles than a military leader: the Messiah, not less than the prophets, belongs to the sphere of miracles, not of politics. Abravanel's Messianology as well as his prophetology are essentially unpolitical doctrines.[1] Now these unpolitical doctrines belong, as it were, to the framework of what Abravanel himself would have called his political teaching, i.e. of his discussion of the best form of human government as distinguished from divine government. Since the unpolitical framework was to Abravanel doubtless incomparably more important than its political content, and since, besides, the understanding of the former is indispensable for the right appreciation of the latter, it will be proper for us to describe the background of his political teaching somewhat more exactly than we have done up to now. That background is not only of an unpolitical, but even of an antipolitical character. As has been shown recently by Professor Baer,[2] Abravanel takes over from Seneca's 90th letter the criticism there developed of human civilization in general (of the

[1] Restating the genuine teaching of the Bible against Maimonides' rationalistic and therefore political teaching, Abravanel goes sometimes farther in the opposite direction than does the Bible itself. The most striking example of this which occurs to me is his interpretation of Judges I, 19: Judah "could not drive out the inhabitants of the valley, because they had chariots of iron". Abravanel explains this passage in the following way: "Judah could not drive out the inhabitants of the valley, *not* because they had chariots of iron."

As regards the difference between Maimonides' political teaching and Abravanel's unpolitical teaching, I have to emphasize the following example. According to Maimonides, the main reason for the fact (told in Exod. XIII, 17 f.) that God did not lead Israel on the direct way, through Philistia, to Palestine, was His intention of educating them in courage (*Guide*, Pt. III, ch. 24, p. 53 *a*, and ch. 32, pp. 70 *b*–71 *a*); according to Abravanel, on the other hand, the main reason was His intention to divide the sea for Israel and to drown the Egyptians (and there was no sea on the way through Philistia); see commentary on the passage (f. 125, cols. 1–2).

[2] *Loc. cit.* pp. 248–53. I have to make only some slight additions to the ample evidence adduced by Baer. (*a*) Abravanel's description of the innocent life in the first period as a life "in the field" (Baer, p. 252) is literally taken over from Seneca, ep. 90 (§42, *agreste domicilium*). (*b*) Abravanel uses in his commentary on Gen. XI, 1 ff. (f. 42, col. 2) the doctrine of Poseidonios, discussed by Seneca, of the government of the best and wisest men in the Golden Age, in a modified form; he says that in the first period of the world, Divine Providence extended itself without any intermediary over mankind, and that, therefore, there were then always wise men, versed in theology. Cp. also Seneca, ep. 90, 44. (*c*) The criticism of Cain as the first founder of the city (Baer, 251) is to be found also in Josephus, *Ant.* I, §62. (*d*) Abravanel uses the general criticism of civilization

"artificial" and "superfluous" things) and of the city in particular. Following Josephus and the Christian Fathers, he combines that Hellenistic teaching with the teaching, in important respects similar, of the first chapters of Genesis. He conceives of urban life and of coercive government, as well as of private property, as productions of human rebellion against the natural order instituted by God: the only life in accordance with nature is a state of liberty and equality of all men, and the possession in common of the natural goods, or, as he seems to suggest at another place,[1] the life "in the field", of independent families. This criticism of all political, "artificial" life does not mean that Abravanel intends to replace the conception of the city as of something "artificial" by the conception of the nation as of something "natural"; for, according to Abravanel, the existence of nations, i.e. the disruption of the one human race into a plurality of nations, is not less "artificial", not less a result of sin, than is the existence of cities.[2] Thus, his criticism of political organization is truly all-comprehensive. And the ultimate reason of this anti-political view is Abravanel's anti-rationalism, the predominance in his thought of the belief in miracles. It is true he accepts the classical teaching of man's "natural" way of life in the beginning, in the Golden Age. But that "natural" state is understood by Abravanel to be of an essentially miraculous character.[3] It is highly significant that he finds an analogy of man's "natural" state in the life led by Israel in the desert,[4] where Israel had to rely entirely for everything

most properly in his interpretation of Exod. xx, 25 (f. 143, col. 1). (e) The distinction between the three ways of life (the bestial, the political, and the theoretical life) (Baer, 251) is obviously taken from Aristotle, *Eth. Nic.* 1095*b*, 17 ff. That distinction had been applied to the three sons of Adam, in the same way as it is by Abravanel, by Maimonides; see *Guide*, Pt. II, ch. 30 and Ephodi's commentary. [1] Commentary on Gen. XI, 1 ff. (f. 41, cols. 1–2).
[2] *Ibid.* (f. 42, cols. 1–2). According to Abravanel's usage, "nation" often has the meaning of "religious community"; he speaks, for example, of the "Christian nation" (see e.g. *Ma'yene hay-Yeshu'ah*, XI, 8, and commentary on I Kings xv, 6, f. 250, col. 3).
[3] Cp. p. 109, n. 2*b* above, with commentary on Josh. x, 12 (f. 21, col. 3).
[4] Commentary on Gen. XI, 1 ff. (f. 41. col. 3). Cp. also commentary on Exod. XVIII, 13–27 (f. 134, col. 2) on the connection between the absence of slavery among the Israelites while they were wandering through the desert (i.e. between their being then in a state of "natural" equality) and their miraculous maintenance by the manna.

PLATE IV

R. ISAACI ABARBANELIS
D I S S E R T A T I O
D E
STATU ET JURE REGIO.

EXCERPTA EX EJUS COMMENTARIO

Ad Deuter. cap. XVII. *verf.* 14. 20. *& ad* 1. *Sam. cap.* VIII.

Ex Hebraico Latine reddita

A JOHANNE BUXTORFIO FILIO.

Reproduced from the Catalogue of the Abravanel Exhibition at the JÜDISCHES MUSEUM *in Berlin, by kind permission of Dr Alfred Klee*

Abravanel's Dissertation on kingship (Deut. XVII, 14–20; I Sam. VIII), with Latin translation by J. Buxtorf junior, from Ugolini, *Thesaurus Antiquitatum*, Venice, 1761.

on miraculous providence. Abravanel, as it were, interprets the "life in the fields", praised by Seneca and the Bucolics, in the spirit of Jeremiah's words (II, 2): "I remember for thee the kindness of thy youth, the love of thine espousals; how thou wentest after me in the wilderness, in a land that was not sown." The "natural" state of mankind is in principle not less miraculous than the Messianic age in which that natural state is to be restored. Maimonides, who held, to say the least, a rather hesitating attitude towards miracles, had adopted, without making any reservation apart from those made by Aristotle himself, the Aristotelian principle that man is naturally a political being; Abravanel, on the other hand, who unhesitatingly accepts all the miracles of the past and of the future, judges of man's political existence as being sinful in its origin, and not instituted, but only, as it were, reluctantly conceded to man, by God.[1] And, he goes on to say, it is with the political and urban life as with the king.[2] That is to say, Abravanel's political teaching, his discussion of the value of monarchy, or, more generally, of the best form of human government, to which I am turning now, is only an application, if the most interesting application, of his fundamental conception, which is strictly anti-political.

Abravanel deals with the question of the best form of human government in his commentaries both on Deut. XVII, 14 f., i.e. on the law which seems to command to Israel the institution of a king, and to I Sam. VIII, 6 f., i.e. on the narration that God and the prophet Samuel were offended by the fact that Israel did ask Samuel for a king.[3] The question is for Abravanel thus primarily an exegetical one: how are the two apparently opposed passages of the Bible to be reconciled? Proceeding

[1] Bound by Gen. II, 18, however, he occasionally adopts that Aristotelian proposition. See Baer, *loc. cit.* pp. 249 f.
[2] Commentary on Gen. XI, 1 ff. (f. 41, col. 3).
[3] The treatment of the question is in both versions (in the earlier version in the commentary on I Sam. VIII, 6 f. (f. 91, col. 2 f. 93, col. 4), and in the later version in the commentary on Deut. XVII, 14 f. (f. 295, col. 2 f. 296, col. 2)) identical as regards the tendency, and even, to a large extent, literally identical. The earlier version is the more important as regards the details of the criticism of kingship; but only the later version provides us with an insight into Abravanel's conception of the ideal government as a whole: his explanation of Deut. XVII, 14 f. is only the continuation of his statements concerning the government of the Jewish nation in general, which are to be found

in the scholastic way, Abravanel begins with surveying and criticizing the earlier attempts, made by Jews and Christians,[1] to solve that exegetical problem. He shows that all those attempts, in spite of their divergencies, and apart from the individual deficiencies of each of them, are based on one and the same decisive assumption. All the earlier commentators mentioned by Abravanel assumed that Israel's asking for a king was a sin, not as such, but only because of the manner or circumstances of their demand. In other words, those commentators presupposed that Deut. XVII, 14 f. expresses a Divine command to institute a king. This, however, includes the further presupposition that monarchy is a good, nay, that it is the best form of human government; for God would not have given His nation any political constitution but the best. Consequently, Abravanel has to discuss first whether monarchy is indeed the best form of human government, and secondly, whether the meaning of Deut. XVII, 14 f. is that Israel is commanded to institute a king.

The first discussion is a criticism, based on reason only, of the monarchist teaching of *the* philosophers, i.e. of Aristotle[2] and his medieval followers. That discussion is, unfortunately, far from being of scholastic orderliness and precision.[3] But the main argument is quite clear. The philosophers who are criticized by Abravanel asserted the necessity of monarchic government by comparing the relation of the king to the political community with the relation of the heart to the human body, and with the relation of the First Cause to the universe.[4] Against such kinds of proof Abravanel objects that

in his interpretation of Deut. XVI, 18 ff. These statements have not been taken into account by Baer, nor by Ephraim E. Urbach, "Die Staatsauffassung des Don Isaak Abrabanel", *Monatsschrift für Geschichte und Wissenschaft des Judentums*, 1937, pp. 257–70, who come, therefore, to conclusions more or less different from those set forth in the present article.

[1] The three opinions of Christian commentators, which are dealt with in the earlier version, are not, however, discussed in the later version.

[2] See commentary on I Sam. VIII, 6 f. (f. 92, col. 1).

[3] It has been made somewhat more lucid in the later version.

[4] Those comparisons were known to Abravanel not only from Christian sources, but also and primarily from Jewish and Islamic ones. In his commentary on Exod. XVIII, 13–27 (f. 134, col. 2) he expressly refers to Fârâbî's *Principles of the beings* (i.e. to the Hebrew translation of *k. al-siyyâsât al-madaniyya*)

they are based on a μετάβασις εἰς ἄλλο γένος, on a μετάβασις from things natural and necessary to things merely possible and subject to the human will. Those philosophers tried, further, to prove the necessity of monarchic government by contending that the three indispensable conditions of well-ordered government are fulfilled only in a monarchy. Those conditions are: unity, continuity, and absolute power. As regards unity, Abravanel states that it may well be achieved by the consent of many governors.[1] As regards continuity, he doubts whether the annual change of governors, who have to answer for their conduct of public affairs after the expiration of their office, and who are, therefore, restrained by "fear of flesh and blood" (*Mora' Basar wa-Dham*) and by their being ashamed of their crimes becoming publicly denounced and punished, is not much to be preferred to the irresponsible, though continuous, government of one. As regards absolute power, Abravanel denies altogether that it is indispensable or desirable: the power of the governors ought to be limited by the laws. He adduces, further, in favour of the government of many, the principle of majority, as accepted by the Jewish law in matters of the interpretation of the law, and the statement made by Aristotle "in the beginning of the *Metaphysics*" that the truth is more easily reached by the collaboration of many than by the exertions of one.[2] After having thus disposed of the philosophic arguments in favour of monarchy, Abravanel turns to the teaching of experience; for, as Aristotle "has taught us", "experience prevails over the syllogism". Now the experience

as proving the necessity of hierarchy leading up to one chief, and in the sentence immediately following that reference, he mentions the examples of the hierarchy in the human body, and of the universal hierarchy which leads up to the First Cause. (Cp. Fârâbî, *loc. cit.* ed. Hyderabad, 1346, H., p. 54, and *Musterstaat*, ed. Dieterici, pp. 54 ff. See also Maimonides, *Guide*, Pt. I, ch. 72.) In the passage mentioned, Abravanel accepts those examples and the monarchist consequence derived from them, while he rejects them in his commentary on Deut. XVII, 14 f. and on I Sam. VIII, 6 f.

[1] Cp. Marsilius of Padua, *Defensor pacis*, lib. I, cap. 15, §2.
[2] The passage which Abravanel has in mind is the beginning of A ἔλ. (993*a*, 30 ff.). I wonder why he did not quote such more suitable passages as *Politics*, III, 16 (1287*b*), and VII, 14 (1332*b*–1333*a*). It may be that he knew the *Politics* only from quotations.

of the present shows that such states as Venice, Florence,[1] Genoa, Lucca, Siena, Bologna and others, which are governed, not by monarchs, but by "judges" elected for limited periods of office, are much superior to the monarchies, as regards both administration of justice and military achievements. And the experience of the past teaches that Rome, when governed by Consuls, conquered the world, while it declined under the emperors. In eloquent sentences which betray a deep hatred of kings and their ways, Abravanel contrasts the admirable character of classical or modern republics with the horrors of monarchies. He arrives at the conclusion that the existence of a king is not only not necessary for a political community, but that it is even an enormous danger and a great harm to it, and that the origin of kingdoms is not the free election of the king by the people, but force and violence.[2]

In spite of his strong indictment of monarchic government,

[1] Cp. Lionardo Bruni's *Oratio in funere Nannis Strozae* (in Baluzius, *Miscellanea*, III, pp. 230 ff.): "Forma reipublicae gubernandae utimur ad libertatem paritatemque civium maxime omnium directa: quae quia aequalissima in omnibus est, popularis nuncupatur. Neminem unum quasi dominum horremus, non paucorum potentiae inservimus.... Monarchiae laus veluti ficta quaedam et umbratilis (est), non autem expressa et solida.... Nec multum secus accidit in dominatu paucorum. Ita popularis una relinquitur legitima reipublicae gubernandae forma, in qua libertas vera sit, in qua aequitas juris cunctis pariter civibus, in qua virtutum studia vigere absque suspicione possint.... Ingeniis vero ac intelligentia sic valent cives nostri ut in ea quidem laude pares non multi, qui vero anteponendi sint, nulli reperiantur. Acritas quidem inest atque industria, et in rebus agendis celeritas et agilitas, animique magnitudo rebus sufficiens. Nec in moderanda republica solum nec in domestica tantum disciplina... valemus, sed etiam bellica gloria insignes sumus. Nam majores quidem nostri... finitimos omnes populos virtute bellica superarunt.... Nostra semper civitas... scientissimos rei militaris duces procreavit."

[2] Cp. John of Salisbury, *Policraticus*, lib. IV, cap. 11: "Regum scrutare historiam, ad hoc petitum regem a Deo invenies, ut praecederet faciem populi. ... Qui tamen non fuerat necessarius, nisi et Israel praevaricatus esset in similitudinem gentium, ut Deo rege sibi non videretur esse contentus.... Hospitem meum Placentinum dixisse recolo... hoc in civitatibus Italiae usu frequenti celeberrimum esse, quod dum pacem diligunt, et iustitiam colunt, et periuriis abstinent, tantae libertatis et pacis gaudio perfruuntur, quod nihil est omnino, quod vel in minimo quietem eorum concutiat.... Adiiciebat etiam quod merita populi omnem evacuant principatum, aut eum faciunt esse mitissimum...." *Ibid.* lib. VIII, cap. 17: "Nisi enim iniquitas, et iniustitia... tyrannidem procurasset, omnino regna non essent, quae... iniquitas aut per se praesumpsit, aut extorsit a domino."

Abravanel no less strongly contends that, if in a country a monarchy exists, the subjects are bound to strict obedience to the king. He informs us that he has not seen in the writings of Jews a discussion of the question whether the people has the right to rebel against the king, or to depose him in case the king becomes a tyrant, and that the Christian scholars who did discuss that question, decided that the people had such a right, according to the classical precedent of the defection of the ten tribes from Rehoboam. Abravanel, who had spoken about this subject "before kings with their wise men", judges that the people has no right to rebellion or deposition, even if the king commits every crime. For the people has, when crowning the king, made a covenant with him by which it promised to him obedience; "and that covenant and oath was not conditional, but absolute; and, therefore, he who rebels against the king is guilty of death, whether the king is righteous or wicked; for it is not the people that inquires into the king's righteousness or wickedness". Besides, the king represents God; he is an image of God as regards both absolute power (the extra-legal actions of the king correspond to the miracles) and unity (the king is unique in his kingdom, as God is unique in His universe). The king is, therefore, entitled to a kind of honour which has something in common with the honour owed by man to God. Consequently, any attempt on the side of the people to depose or to punish their king, is in a sense sacrilegious.[1] It is obvious that the second argument is contradictory to the assertions made by Abravanel two or three pages earlier, in his discussion of the value of monarchy. It would, however, be unfair perhaps to so prolific a writer as Abravanel, to attach too much stress to his inconsistencies; and in particular to the present inconsistency.[2] For if the second argument used

---

[1] Commentary on Deut. xvii, 16–20 (f. 296, col. 4; f. 297, col. 1). Abravanel further adduces a third argument which, however, applies to Jewish kings only. Cp. also his commentaries on Judges iv, 9 (f. 46, col. 1); on I Kings ii, 37 (f. 202, col. 3); on I Kings xiii, 2 (f. 246, col. 1); and on I Kings xii passim.
[2] Cp. also above, p. 112, n. 4. Another example of this kind of inconsistency may be mentioned in passing. In his commentary on I Sam. viii, 7 (f. 93, col. 4),

by him in support of his thesis, that the people has no right to depose or punish a tyrannous king, is inconsistent with his denial of the value of monarchy, the thesis itself is perfectly consistent with his main contention, that monarchy, as such, is an enormous danger and a great evil.

Was, then, the political ideal of Abravanel the republic? He does not use a word which could be translated by "republic"; the kind of government which he praises is called by him government of "many". This is very vague indeed. The statements occurring in his criticism of monarchy might convey the impression that his ideal was democracy. But, as we shall see later, he accepted the doctrine of the necessity of a "mixed" constitution. Thus, his ideal cannot have been a "pure" constitution of any kind. I believe we would not be wide of the mark if we defined his political ideal by saying that it was, like that of Calvin[1] one or two generations later, an "aristocracy near to democracy".[2] But in order to avoid any hypothesis, we shall do best to confine ourselves to the statement that Abravanel's political ideal was the republic. For "republic" is a term of a polemic and negative character; it does not say more than "not monarchy", without defining whether that non-monarchical government desired is democratic, aristocratic, oligarchic, and so on.[3] And what Abravanel says of the best form of human government is hardly more than just this: that it is unmonarchical.

But was the political ideal of Abravanel really the republican city-state? That this was the case is most unlikely from the outset. If it were the case, it would betray not only inconsistency—inconsistent Abravanel admittedly was—but even an almost insane looseness of thought. Indeed, it is

i.e. only two or three pages after he had finished the proof that the existence of a king is not necessary in any nation, Abravanel says: "the king is necessary for the other nations" (for all nations except Israel).

[1] *Institutio*, lib. IV, cap. 20, §8 (with regard to the Jewish commonwealth).

[2] The aristocratic element in the ideal constitution, as conceived by Abravanel, i.e. of the Jewish constitution, is the *Synhedrion* of 70. Cp. also commentary on Exod. XVIII, 13–27 (f. 134, col. 3). Abravanel's ideal is characterized as "*status aristocraticus*" by Menasseh ben Israel, *Conciliator*, qu. 6, ad Deut. (Frankfort, 1633, p. 227).

[3] Cp. Montesquieu's definition in *De l'esprit des lois*, livre II, ch. 1.

inconceivable that the very man who, in accordance with his deepest theological convictions, judged the city to be the work of human wickedness, should have been at the same time a genuine and unreserved admirer of the worldly greatness of Rome and Venice. One cannot explain the contradiction by supposing that Abravanel was merely a humanist orator who was able to devote eloquent sentences to any subject. For, eloquent though he could be, he certainly was no sophist: he had a strong and sincere belief in the one truth. The only possible explanation is that Abravanel's admiration for the classical and modern city-states was not more than a tribute which he paid to the fashion of his time; that it was a side-track into which he was guided occasionally, if on more than one occasion, by the influence of humanism, but primarily by his disgust at kings and their worldly splendour, which had a deeper root than the humanist influence.

Before beginning to define the true character of Abravanel's political ideal, let us emphasize the fact that the exaltation of the republican city-state belongs to the discussion, based on reason only, of the best form of human government, i.e. to a mere prelude to the central discussion of it, which is based on the Scripture only. After what has been said about Abravanel's philosophical tendency, there is no need for a further proof of the assertion that only his interpretation of the teaching of the Scripture can provide us with his authentic conception of the ideal form of human government. What, then, does the Scripture teach concerning the human government of Israel? This question is answered by Abravanel both precisely and lucidly. He begins by stating his thesis, which runs as follows: Even if he granted that the king is useful and necessary in all other nations for the ordering of the political community and for its protection—which, however, he does not grant, but even vigorously denies—even in that case the king would certainly not be necessary for the Jewish nation. For their king is God, and, therefore, they need, even incomparably less than the other nations, a king of flesh and blood. A king could be necessary for three purposes: for military leadership, for legislation, and for extraordinary power to punish

the wicked. All those purposes are achieved in Israel in the
most perfect way by God, who vouchsafes His particular
providence to His elected nation. Thus, a king is not necessary
in Israel. He is even most dangerous in Israel. Experience
has shown that all the kings of Israel and most of the kings of
Judah led Israel and Judah into idolatry, while the judges
and the prophets were, all of them, godfearing men. This
proves that the leadership of "judges" is good, while that of
kings is bad. The result, at which the discussion based on
reason only had arrived, is confirmed by the scrutiny of the
Scripture, and particularly of the biblical narratives. More
exactly, that result has undergone, as a consequence of the
scrutiny of the Bible, an important precision, which is, at the
same time, an important correction: the ideal form of human
government is not the republic as such, but a "republican"
government, instituted and guided by God.[1]

Arrived at this point, Abravanel has yet to overcome the
greatest difficulty. The earlier Jewish commentators, whose
views he had criticized to begin with, were no less familiar
with the innumerable passages of the Bible which attribute
the kingship to God, than he himself was. They also remembered, no less well than he did, the evil which Israel and
Judah had experienced under their wicked kings. But they
remembered also the deeds and words of such godfearing
kings as David, the author of many Psalms, as Solomon, the
author of the Song of Songs, and as Jotham, Hezekiah, and
Josiah, who were "saints of the Highest".[2] And, even more
important than this, the Messiah for whose speedy coming
they prayed, was conceived of by them as a king. Now, as
regards the last point, Abravanel was consistent enough to
deny that the Messiah is a king properly speaking: the
Messiah, too, is, according to him, not a king, but a prophet
and a judge.[3] But this conception of the leadership of the
Messiah is already based on the truly decisive assumption

---

[1] See also Urbach, *loc. cit.* pp. 263 f.
[2] Cp. Abravanel's Introduction to his commentary on the Books of the Kings
(f. 188, col. 3).
[3] See Baer, *loc. cit.* p. 259.

that the institution of a king in Israel was not expressly commanded by God. The earlier commentators were convinced that Deut. xvii, 14 f. did express such a command. As long as the difficulty offered by that passage was not overcome, all other passages of the Bible which Abravanel might adduce in support of his thesis were of little weight. For none of those other passages contained a definite law concerning the institution of kingship in Israel.

Abravanel denies that Deut. xvii, 14 f. expresses a command to institute a king in Israel. According to him, that passage merely gives permission to do this. We need not examine whether his interpretation is right or not. What matters for us is, that the interpretation rejected by Abravanel was accepted as legally binding by Jewish tradition, which was, as a rule, decidedly in favour of monarchy. The traditional interpretation had been accepted in particular by Maimonides, who had embodied it in his great legal work as well as in his *Sepher ham-Miṣvoth*.[1]

According to the interpretation accepted by the Jewish tradition, Deut. xvii, 14 f. would have to be translated as follows:

When thou art come unto the land which the Lord thy God giveth thee, and shalt possess it, and shalt dwell therein; and shalt

[1] It was accepted also, for example, by Naḥmanides, Moses of Coucy, Gersonides, and Bachya ben Asher. (This is not to deny that Gersonides' and Bachya's statements in their commentaries on Deut. xvii, 14 f. are almost as much anti-monarchistic as those of Abravanel—there are a number of important literal concords between the statements of Abravanel and those of both Gersonides and Bachya—but still, both of them interpret the passage in question as conveying a command to institute a king.) As far as I know, the only Jewish medieval commentator who, in his commentary on Deut. xvii, 14 f., expressly understands that passage as conveying a permission is Ibn Ezra. The exceptional character of Abravanel's interpretation is implicitly recognized by Moses Hayyim Alshekh (*Mar'oth haṣ-Ṣobe'oth*, on I Sam. viii, 6 f.) who vigorously rejects that interpretation by referring himself to the Jewish tradition, and expressly by Menasseh ben Israel (*Conciliator*, ed. cit. p. 228), who says: "*Haec opinio* (sc. *Abravanelis*) *quamvis satis congrua verbis S. Scripturae, a multis tamen accepta non est, quia adversatur sententiae ac traditioni antiquorum.*" Abravanel's interpretation was tacitly accepted by Moses Mendelssohn (*Jerusalem*, Berlin, 1783, ii, pp. 117 ff.), and rejected by S. R. Hirsch and by Buber-Rosenzweig. Cp. also Isaak Heinemann, *Philos. griechische und jüdische Bildung*, Breslau, 1932, pp. 185 f., and Urbach, *loc. cit.* p. 269. (The essay of Heinrich Heinemann in the *Jahrbuch der Jüdisch-literarischen Gesellschaft*, 1916, was not accessible to me.)

say (or:[1] *then thou shalt say*), I will set a king over me, like as all the nations that are round about me; *Thou shalt in any wise set a king over thee.* Thou shalt set him king over thee, whom the Lord Thy God shall choose: one from among thy brethren shalt thou set over thee: thou mayest not put a foreigner over thee, which is not thy brother.

According to Abravanel's interpretation, the passage in question would read as follows:

When thou art come unto the land which the Lord Thy God giveth thee, and shalt possess it, and shalt dwell therein; and shalt say, I will set a king over me, like as all the nations that are round about me; *then thou shalt set him king over thee whom the Lord Thy God shall choose:* one from among thy brethren shalt thou set king over thee: thou mayest not put a foreigner over thee, which is not thy brother.

According to the traditional interpretation, the purport of the law, contained in the passage, is that Israel is commanded to institute a king. According to Abravanel's interpretation, its purport is that, *if* Israel wishes to institute a king—and to do this, Israel is by the law implicitly permitted, but permitted only—then Israel may do it only in such and such a manner. Now Abravanel's interpretation, which is directly opposed to that of the Jewish tradition, is in substance identical with that implied in the Vulgate.[2] Abravanel is, of course, much more explicit than the Vulgate can be.[3] And, apart from this, he goes much further than the Latin transla-

---

[1] According to Naḥmanides.

[2] "Cum ingressus fueris terram, quam Dominus Deus tuus dabit tibi, et possederis eam, habitaverisque in illa, et dixeris: Constituam super me regem, sicut habent omnes per circuitum nationes; *eum constitues, quem Dominus tuus elegerit de numero fratrum tuorum....*" Cp. also the English translation: "...Thou shalt in any wise set *him* king over thee, whom the Lord thy God shall choose...."

[3] It will be proper to give a more complete (if partially free) rendering of Abravanel's interpretation by putting his explanatory remarks on the biblical words into brackets. He explains: "When thou art come unto the land which the Lord Thy God giveth thee, and shalt possess it, and shalt dwell therein [i.e. it will be foolish that in the time of the wars, during the conquest of the land, you will not ask for a king; for this would be the most proper time for the need for a king; but after you will possess the land, and you will have divided it, and you will dwell in it in safety, and this will have happened by the providence o. God, without there being then a king—then, without any necessity and need whatsoever] thou shalt say, I will set a king over me [namely] like as all the nations that are round about me [i.e. for no other necessity and purpose (but

tion does. He says, explaining the passage in question more precisely:

(When thou shalt wish to do this), in spite of its not being proper, (thou mayest not do it but in such and such a manner). This is similar to the section of the law which runs as follows: When thou goest forth to battle against thine enemies, and the Lord thy God deliverest them into thine hands...and seest among the captives a beautiful woman, and thou hast a desire unto her....For there the precept is not that he shall desire her, and not that he shall take her to him to wife..., since this is permitted only, and an effect of the wicked inclination. But the precept is that, after the first cohabitation, thou shalt bring her home into thine house.... Israel was not commanded in the Torah to ask for a king..., and the king was not necessary and indispensable for the government of their gatherings..., for God was their king truly....Therefore, when Israel asked for a king..., the anger of the Lord was kindled against them, and He said: they have not rejected thee, but they have rejected me, that I should not be king over them; and Samuel said: ye said unto me, Nay, but a king shall reign over us; when the Lord your God was your king. This shows that the sin consisted in their "kicking" at God's kingship and their choosing a human kingship. For this reason, neither Joshua nor the other Judges instituted a king.

The final expression of Abravanel's interpretation is that Deut. xvii, 14 f. contains a permission given "with regard to the wicked inclination" (*Yeṣer ha-Raʿ*). Now this more precise expression, too, is in substance borrowed from a Christian source. That source is the *Postilla* of Nicolas of Lyra.[1] Thus

to assimilate yourselves to the nations of the world); when this will happen], thou shalt [not] set [him] king over thee [whom you wish, but him] whom the Lord Thy God shall choose...." Commentary on I Sam. viii, 6 f. (f. 93, cols. 1–2).

[1] Nicolas says on Deut. xvii, 14 f.: "non est praeceptum, nec simplex concessio, quia sic non peccasset populus Israel petendo regem, cujus contrarium dicitur I Reg. xii: sed est permissio quae est de malo. Bonum enim populi consistebat in hoc, quod solus Deus regnaret super eum, eo quod erat populus peculiaris Dei; veruntamen si importune regem habere vellent, permittebatur eis, sub conditionibus tamen...." This is explained more fully in the *Postilla* on I Reg. viii: "illud quod dicitur Deut. 17 de constitutione regis...non fuit concessio proprie dicta, sed magis permissio, sicut repudium uxoris fuit permissum ad duritiam cordis eorum...." The comparison shows that Abravanel has merely replaced Nicolas' example by the example of the "beautiful woman". But the point of view of Abravanel is identical with that of Nicolas. There is one important difference between the Jewish and the Christian commentator: while Abravanel thinks that monarchy is intrinsically bad, Nicolas is of the

we are entitled to say that Abravanel's interpretation of
Deut. xvii, 14 f., i.e. of the chief biblical passage, or, in other
words, that his opinion concerning the incompatibility of
monarchy with the constitution of Israel, goes immediately
back to Christian, not to Jewish sources.

Generally speaking, both the Jewish and the Christian
tradition, and in particular both the Jewish and the Christian
Middle Ages, were in favour of monarchy. Anti-monarchist
statements are, in both traditions, exceptional up to the
humanist age. Thus one is at a loss to state which of the two
traditions shows a comparatively stronger monarchist (or
anti-monarchist) trend than the other. One could, however,
dare to make such a statement if it were based on a com-

opinion that monarchy is in principle the best form of government. Nicolas only
contests that that which holds true of all other nations, holds equally true of
Israel, the nation governed by God. Only this part of Nicolas' argument has
been taken over by Abravanel. (Cp. the beginning of Abravanel's discussion
concerning monarchy in Israel: "Even if we grant, that the king is most
necessary in the nation for the ordering of the political community...he is not
necessary in the nation of Israel....") Nicolas says on I Reg. viii: "Ad
maiorem praedictorum evidentiam quaeritur, utrum filii Israel peccaverint
petendo super se regem. Et arguitur quod non, quia petere illud quod est bonum
simpliciter, et de dictamine rationis rectae, non est peccatum; gubernatio autem
populi per regem est optima, ut dicit Philosophus 3. Politicorum. et per con-
sequens est de dictamine rationis rectae....Item illud quod conceditur lege
divina licitum est, quia nullum peccatum concedit, sed Deut. 17. c. concedit
lex divina filiis Israel constitutionem regis....[Notice that even in this "monarchist" objection Deut. xvii, 14 f. is understood to contain a *concessio* only.]
Contra infra 12. c. dicitur: Scietis et videbitis....Ad hoc dicendum quod, cum
regnum sit optima politia, caeterae gentes a filiis Israel petendo vel constituendo
super se regem non peccaverunt, sed magis bonum egerunt. Filii autem Israel
hoc faciendo peccaverunt....Cuius ratio est, quia Deus populum Israel elegit
sibi specialem et peculiarem prae caeteris populis...et idem voluit esse rex
immediatus illius populi...propter quod voluit homines gubernatores illius
populi ab ipso immediate institui, tanquam eius vicarii essent, et non reges vel
domini: ut patet in Moyse et Josue, et de iudicibus sequentibus...." (That
Abravanel knew the *Postilla*, is shown by his express quotations from it—see
Guttmann, *loc. cit.* p. 46. But, apart from that, that interpretation given by
earlier commentators of Deut. xvii, 14 f. (or I Sam. viii, 6 f.) which he esteems
most highly and which he discusses most fully, is the interpretation given by
Paulus of Burgos, and this interpretation is to be found in Paulus' *Additiones* to
the *Postilla*.) Cp. further Thomas Aquinas, *Summa theologiae*, ii, 1, qu. 105,
art. 1: "regnum est optimum regimen populi, si non corrumpatur. Sed...de
facili regnum degenerat in tyrannidem...ideo *Dominus a principio* (Judaeis)
regem non instituit cum plena potestate, sed judicem et gubernatorem in eorum
custodiam; sed postea regem ad petitionem populi *quasi indignatus concessit*, ut
patet per hoc quod dixit ad Samuel I Reg. 8, 7....Instituit tamen a principio

parison of comparable magnitudes, i.e. of a Jewish source
which is at the same time authoritative and popular, with the
corresponding Christian source. Now if we compare the
manner in which the Jewish Bible on the one hand (i.e. the
Targum Onḳelos, the Targum Jonathan, and the commentaries of Rashi, Ibn Ezra and Naḥmanides), and the Christian
(Latin) Bible on the other (i.e. the *Glossa interlinearis*, the
Glossa ordinaria, the *Postilla* of Nicolas of Lyra, and the
Additiones of Paulus Burgensis) deal with the chief passage, i.e.
with the law concerning the institution of a king, we find that
the Jewish Bible shows not the slightest sign of an anti-
monarchist tendency,[1] while the Christian Bible exhibits a
definite anti-monarchist trend, based on theocratic assumptions.[2] The only exception to this rule in the Christian Bible

circa regem instituendum, primo quidem modum eligendi....Secundo ordi-
navit circa reges institutos...." The fact that the kings had absolute power,
while the power of the judges was more limited, is stressed by Abravanel in the
introduction to his commentary on Judges (f. 40, col. 1). Cp. also John of
Salisbury, *Policraticus*, lib. viii, cap. 18: "...primi patres et patriarchae vivendi
ducem optimum naturam secuti sunt. Successerunt duces a Moyse sequentes
legem, et iudices qui legis auctoritate regebant populum; et eosdem fuisse
legimus sacerdotes. Tandem in furore Domini dati sunt reges, alii quidem boni,
alii vero mali...populus...a Deo, quem contempserat, sibi regem extorsit...
(Saul) tamen christus Domini dictus est, et tirannidem exercens regium non
amisit honorem...." With this passage, the whole of Abravanel's political
teaching should be compared. As regards the later development, I would refer
the reader particularly to Milton, *Pro populo Anglicano defensio contra Salmasii
Defensionem Regiam*, cap. 2. It is interesting in our connection to observe that,
while Salmasius (*Defensio Regia*, cap. 2) makes ample use of the rabbinic interpretations of Deut. xvii, 14 f. (and of I Sam. viii) for the proof of his royalist
thesis, Milton much prefers Josephus to the "tenebrionibus Rabbinis" (cp. on
Josephus below, p. 127).
[1] The Targum Onḳelos renders the passage literally. The Targum Jonathan
renders the words "Thou shalt in any wise set a king over thee, whom the Lord
thy God shall choose: one from among thy brethren shalt thou set king over
thee", in the following way: "You shall inquire for instruction before the Lord,
and afterwards appoint the king over you." Rashi does not say anything on the
passage. Ibn Ezra simply says that the passage expresses a permission, Naḥmanides conceives of it as containing a command to ask for a king and to
institute a king.
[2] The *Glossa interlinearis* remarks on "et dixeris": "Tu non ego," and on
"Constituam super me regem": "Non Deum sed hominem." The *Glossa
ordinaria* (Augustinus, qu. 26) says: "Quaeri potest cur displicuit populus Deo,
cum regem desideravit, cum hic inveniatur esse permissus? Sed intelligendum
est merito non fuisse secundum voluntatem Dei, quia hoc fieri non praecepit
sed desiderantibus permisit." As regards the *Postilla*, see above. Paulus
Burgensis says: "Praeceptum istud de constitutione regis non est permissive

is the explanation of the passage in question given by Paulus of Burgos, i.e. by a baptized Jew. The result of this comparison confirms our impression that the immediate origin of Abravanel's anti-monarchist conclusions from his theocratic premises has to be sought for, not in Jewish, but in Christian sources.

Of Christian origin is, above all, Abravanel's general conception of the government of the Jewish nation. According to him, that government consists of two kinds of governments, of a government human and of a government spiritual or divine. This distinction is simply the Christian distinction between the authority spiritual and the authority temporal. Abravanel further divides each of these two governments into three degrees. As regards the government human, the lowest degree is the "little *Beth-Din*", i.e. the court of justice of every town. The members of those courts are elected by the people. The second degree of the government human is the "great *Beth-Din*", i.e. the *Synhedrion* in Jerusalem. The members of the *Synhedrion* are not elected by the people, but nominated either by the king, or, if there is no king, by the president of the *Synhedrion*, after consultation with the other members; the president himself is chosen by the members of the *Synhedrion*. This body, being an image of the seventy elders led by Moses, consists of seventy-one persons. The highest place in human government is occupied by the king. The king is chosen by God, not by the people, who have, therefore, no right whatsoever to rebel against the king or to depose him. The office of the king is not the administration of justice, but, in the first instance, military leadership, and then the extra-judicial punishment of the wicked in cases of urgency. His claim to obedience and honour is stressed by Abravanel scarcely less than it is by Maimonides; in this respect both alike are simply following Jewish tradition.[1] If one takes into

intelligendum...sed est simplex concessio cum conditionibus in litera scriptis. Nec sequitur quod si sit concessio simplex, tunc non pecasset populus Israel petendo regem. Nam petierunt regem aliter quam fuit sibi concessum."

[1] Commentary on Deut. xvi, 18–xvii, 1, and on xvii, 8–15 (f. 293, cols. 1–2; f. 294, col. 1; f. 296, cols. 2–3). Cp. commentary on I Kings i (f. 196, col. 4) and Introduction to commentary on Judges (f. 39, col. 3, f. 40, col. 1). In the

account Abravanel's criticism of monarchy in general and of monarchy in Israel in particular, one has to define his view concerning the highest degree of human government in the Jewish nation more exactly by saying that the chief of that government is, according to the original intention of the legislator, not a king properly speaking, but a leader of the kind that Moses and the Judges were. As a matter of fact, Abravanel expressly states that "the first king who reigned over Israel" was Moses.[1] At any rate, the human government of the Jewish nation, as Abravanel sees it, consists of a monarchic element (Moses and his successors), of an aristocratic element (the Sanhedrin), and of a democratic element (the local judges elected by the people). It is a "mixed" government, in full accordance with the classical doctrine. The immediate source of this view of Abravanel is again a Christian one: Thomas Aquinas' description of the Jewish constitution in the *Summa theologiae*,[2] which has been altered by Abravanel only in detail. So much about Abravanel's conception of the government human. As regards the government spiritual, he again distinguishes three degrees: the prophet, who is the chief; the priests; and, in the lowest category, the Levites.[3] This distinction implies that the

commentary on Deut. XVI, 18–XVII, 13 (f. 293, col. 2 and f. 294, col. 2) Abravanel says, however, that the extraordinary power of jurisdiction belongs, not to the king, but to the *Synhedrion*. Following the ruling of the Jewish tradition, he points out that all appointments in Israel are for life, and, in principle, hereditary (*loc. cit.* f. 293, col. 2). In his "rational" discussion of the best form of human government, he showed a definite preference for short periods of office.

[1] Commentary on I Kings 1 (f. 196, col. 4). See also commentary on Exod. XVIII, 13–27 (f. 134, col. 1).

[2] II, 1, qu. 105, art. 1. Thomas defines the character of the government instituted by the *lex vetus* by calling that government a "politia bene commixta ex regno, inquantum unus praeest, ex aristocratia, inquantum multi principantur secundum virtutem, et ex democratia, id est, potestate populi, inquantum ex popularibus possunt eligi principes, et ad populum pertinet electio principum. Et hoc fuit institutum secundum legem divinam; nam Moyses et ejus successores (*sc.* Josua, Judices, et reges) gubernabant populum, quasi singulariter omnibus principantes, quod est *quaedam species regni*. Eligebantur autem septuaginta duo seniores secundum virtutem...et hoc erat aristocraticum. Sed democraticum erat quod isti de omni populo eligebantur...." Cp. also the passage from the same article quoted above, p. 121, n. 1.

[3] Commentary on Deut. XVI, 18–XVII, 1 (f. 293, col. 1), and on XVIII, 1–8 (f. 297, cols. 1–2).

hierarchy spiritual, not less than the hierarchy human, leads up to a monarchical head. In this, again, Abravanel is following the teaching of the Christian Middle Ages, according to which the government of the whole church must be monarchical: he merely replaces Petrus (or his successors) by the prophet.[1] The government spiritual, as conceived by Abravanel, is, of course, not purely monarchical; it contains also an aristocratic and, perhaps, a democratic element. This view of the spiritual hierarchy is also borrowed from Christians.[2] And it is for Abravanel no less a matter of course than it is for the papalist writers among the Christians, that human government, and, in particular, government by kings, which was not instituted by, but extorted from God, is much inferior in dignity to the government spiritual. And, besides, the aristocratic element of the human government of the Jewish nation, the *Synhedrion*, consists, as Abravanel points out, mainly of priests and Levites.[3] The ideal commonwealth, as understood by Abravanel, is governed mainly by prophets and priests; and the ideal leader is for him not, as for Maimonides, a philosopher king, but a priest king.[4] His political ideal is of a strictly hierocratic character. He was, as far as I know, the first Jew who became deeply influenced by Christian political thought. It deserves to be stressed that he adopted the views of the extreme papalists. He had preferred Christian scholasticism to the philosophy of the Jewish rationalists, and he arrived at a political ideal which was nearer to the ideal of Gregory VII[5] and Innocent III than to that of Maimonides. He had undermined Maimonides' political philosophy of the law by contesting its ultimate

---

[1] Cp. Thomas Aquinas, *Summa contra Gentiles*, lib. iv, cap. 76.

[2] Bellarmin, *De Romano Pontifice*, lib. i, cap. 5: "Jam vero doctores catholici conveniunt omnes, ut regimen ecclesiasticum hominibus a Deo commissum, sit illud quidem monarchicum, sed temperatum...ex aristocratia et dimocratia."

[3] Commentary on Deut. xvii, 8–13 (f. 294, col. 2–3).

[4] Commentary on I Kings i (f. 196, col. 4) and on Exod. xviii, 13–27 (f. 134, cols. 1–2). Cp. John of Salisbury, *Policraticus*, lib. viii, cap. 18 (quoted above, p. 121, n. 1) and Augustinus Triumphus, *Summa de potestate ecclesiastica*, Pt. i, qu. 1, art. 7–8.

[5] Cp. with Abravanel's statements those of Gregory VII and others, quoted by Carlyle, *A History of Mediaeval Political Theory in the West*, iii (2nd ed.), pp. 94 and 99.

assumption that the city is "natural", and by conceiving of the city as a product of human sin, i.e. he had started from unpolitical, and even antipolitical premises, and he arrived at the political creed of clericalism.

But however great the influence of Christian medieval thought on Abravanel's political teaching may have been, that influence scarcely accounts for his so-called republicanism. This part of his political creed is not of Christian medieval, but of humanist origin. Humanism means going back from the tradition to the sources of the tradition. *The* sources, however, are for Abravanel, not so much the historians, poets and orators of classical antiquity, but the literal sense of the Bible—and Josephus.[1] Josephus understood Deut. xvii, 14 f. as permitting only, not commanding, the institution of a king. And he unequivocally states that the government instituted by Moses was an aristocracy as opposed to a monarchy.[2] Above all, the ἄριστοι, who govern the Jewish state, are identified by him with the priests, whose chief is the high priest.[3] Thus we conclude that Abravanel's view of the Jewish government as a whole is taken over from Josephus. And by taking into account the result of our previous analysis, we shall sum up by saying that Abravanel restates the aristocratic and anti-monarchist view of Josephus in terms of the Christian distinction between the authority spiritual and the authority temporal.

When speaking of the influence of humanism on Abravanel's political teaching, we have, then, to think not primarily of his "republicanism"—of his admiration for the greatness of republican Rome and for the patriotism of its citizens—which is rather on the surface of his thought. His humanism has indeed hardly anything in common with the "heathenish" humanism of men like Lionardo Bruni. Abravanel is a humanist of the kind represented by Coluccio Salutati, who

---

[1] As regards Abravanel's knowledge of Josephus, see Baer, *loc. cit.* p. 246.
[2] *Ant.* lib. iv, §223, and lib. vi, §35.
[3] See in particular *Contra Apion.*, lib. ii, §§185–8 and 193–4, but also *Ant.* lib. iv, §§218 ("high priest, prophet, and *Synhedrion*") and 224.

might be said to have served as his model.[1] That is to say, he is a humanist who uses his classical learning to confirm his thoroughly medieval conceptions rather than to free himself from them. He is distinguished from the medieval writers rather by the method which he uses than by the views which he expresses. This method may be called historical.[2] Abravanel tends to pay more attention to the sources of the tradition than to the tradition itself. He often urges the difference between the literal sense of the Bible and the Midrashic interpretations; in doing this, he is guided, not as a medieval rationalist might have been, by an opposition to the "mythical" or "mystical" tendencies of the Midrash—for these tendencies are in full accordance with his own deepest inclinations—but by an interest in establishing the pure, undistorted meaning of the divinely inspired text, by an interest not so much in proving that a certain favoured doctrine is revealed, and therefore true, but to know exactly what Revelation teaches, in order to be able to adopt that teaching, whatever it may be. By preferring in this spirit the sources of the tradition to the tradition itself, he can scarcely avoid the danger of coming into conflict with the teaching of tradition. An important example of that criticism of traditional views, which is based on the return to the sources (both the literal sense of the Bible and Josephus), has attracted our attention in the foregoing pages. To the same connection belongs Abravanel's criticism of certain traditional opinions concerning the authorship of some biblical books, a criticism by which he paved the way for the much more thoroughgoing biblical criticism of Spinoza.[3] When considering these and similar facts, we may be inclined to complete our earlier statement that Abravanel's thought was fundamentally determined by the Jewish tradition by adding that his teaching tends to be more of a biblicist than of a traditionalist character. But after having granted this, we must stress all the more that

[1] Cp. Alfred von Martin, *Mittelalterliche Welt- und Lebensanschauung im Spiegel der Schriften Coluccio Salutatis*, Munich und Berlin, 1913, pp. 22, 61 ff., 82 ff., and 97 ff., and the same author's *Coluccio Salutati's Traktat Vom Tyrannen*, Berlin und Leipzig, 1913, pp. 75 ff.   [2] With due caution.

[3] Cp. L. Strauss, *Die Religionskritik Spinozas*, Berlin, 1930, pp. 280 f.

the assumptions of the pre-medieval world to which Abravanel turns back, sometimes by criticizing medieval opinions, are not fundamentally different from the medieval assumptions from which he started. He goes back, it is true, from the monarchist ideal of the Middle Ages to the aristocratic ideal of antiquity. But, as matters stand, this does not mean more than that he goes back from the moderate hierocratic ideal of the Middle Ages to the much more intransigent hierocratic ideal of the period of the Second Temple, as expounded by Josephus. He is distinguished from the Jewish medieval writers by the fact that he is much more clerical than they are.

His descent was, as he believed, royal. His soul was the soul of a priest—of a priest who had not forgotten that the Temple, built by King Solomon in the holy city, was "infinitely inferior in sanctity" to the tabernacle erected by Moses in the desert.[1] Whatever he may have had to learn from the Cynics or from the Bucolics of antiquity as regards the dubious merits of human arts and city life, his knowledge of the sinful origin of cities, and of towers, and of kingdoms, and of the punishment following the eating of the fruit of the tree of knowledge was not borrowed from any foreign source: it was the inheritance of his own race which was commanded to be a kingdom of priests.

[1] Commentary on I Kings VI, 1 (f. 217, col. 3).

Lecture VI

LEONE EBREO AND THE RENAISSANCE

BY A. R. MILBURN

LEONE EBREO AND THE RENAISSANCE

THE date of the birth of Isaac Abravanel's eldest son, Judah, is not known for certain, but it is presumed that he was born about 1460 in Lisbon. Like many Jews of the name of Judah, he was called Leo among Christians and is known to literary historians by the appellation he received in his adopted country: Leone Ebreo. He appears to have been educated very largely by his father who, no doubt, gave most attention to instruction in Jewish philosophy, especially since Jewish culture thrived greatly in Lisbon at that time, causing the synagogue there to rival the great rabbinical schools of Toledo and Cordova. Besides the work of the medieval Jewish and Arabic philosophers, Leone would be educated in ancient and in scholastic philosophy, though ancient philosophy in Portugal, it must be noted, meant the work of Aristotle, for the strife which still raged between Platonists and Aristotelians in Italy had as yet found no echo in the Iberian peninsula.

But besides such general philosophical studies, he was engaged in the special study of medicine, which he made his profession, and in 1483 he was already a doctor in Lisbon in an independent position. Medicine, though, was not merely a profession or a manner of earning a living for Leone. Biological and anatomical observations play a large part in his *Dialoghi*, and geological and astronomical knowledge is a necessary constituent of his theories with regard to the love relationships of all created things. An opportunity for the acquisition of such information was offered by the very wide studies demanded of the medical profession at that time.

In 1483 Isaac Abravanel was implicated in the conspiracy of the Duke of Braganza against João II, and compelled to flee to Seville, where Leone and his two brothers followed him in the next year. Here Leone continued to practise as a doctor. Here, too, he married, and in 1491 a son, Isaac, was born to him. But in the following year, 1492, came the decree expelling the Jews from Spain. The lack of doctors in Spain, which was one of the results of this decree, caused King Ferdinand to attempt to retain the services of Leone, who must already have won much renown in his profession. Leone refused to accept such a favour, whereupon Ferdinand devised the plan of kidnapping Leone's son to enforce his stay. News of this came to Leone's ears and he sent his son secretly into Portugal with his nurse, himself taking ship with his father and the other members of his family for Italy. João II, learning that his enemy's grandson was on Portuguese territory, had him taken and baptized as some measure of revenge.

Again, it is not known for certain whether Leone ever saw his son afterwards, but in the year 1560, Amatus Lusitanus saw in Salonica, in the house of a son of Isaac Abravanel the younger, a book, *De Coeli Harmonia*, written by Leone Ebreo, and which, it is likely, had been given personally by the author to his son.

In 1492 the Abravanel family landed in Naples where there was a flourishing Jewish community and, as their way was, quickly made themselves indispensable to the King, Ferdinand II of Aragon, whose doctor Leone became. And here in Naples he found a Jewish culture which was undoubtedly influenced by the Italian Renaissance, whose chief exponents were Judah ben Yehiel who compiled a Hebrew grammar on a Ciceronian basis and whose every effort was directed to bringing Latin and Jewish thought into harmony with each other; and Elia del Medigo, the friend and assistant of Pico della Mirandola. The culture and aims of men like these were very different from those of the Spanish or Portuguese Jews, brought up upon the scholastic philosophy, the rules of which had dictated the form and methods of the philosophical exposition of Leone's own father. Another great difference lay in the fact that while Spanish-Jewish philosophy continued to be influenced by the rationalism of Maimonides, the thought of Italian Jews fell much more under the sway of the Cabbala, and not of Jews only, but also of Christians, for Pico della Mirandola and many other scholars of the time studied it extensively. It was from the Cabbala that Leone took his description of man as a microcosm.

Another famous Jew Leone may well have known during this period was Yohanan Alemanno, Pico della Mirandola's Hebrew master, and the man to whom Leone may probably have owed his introduction to Pico. There exist certain similarities between the work of Yohanan Alemanno and that of Leone, and especially a formal one which is notable: both use the dialogue form, but the conversation is not divided between several interlocutors, as in the famous Italian dialogues of Bembo, Castiglione and others, but occurs between two people only, whose names represent abstract qualities.

But the leader of intellectual activity in Naples was the great humanist Pontano. All Pontano's devotion was for astrology, and his two great works are both given over to astrological speculation; moreover, he explains ancient myths as astrological allegories. Now almost the whole of the second of Leone's *Dialoghi* is likewise devoted to such speculation, and again ancient myths are considered as astrological allegories. This would be remarkable in one brought up upon Jewish philosophy (for which a gulf, which cannot be bridged, exists between God and all created things), and can be ascribed only to the influence of Pontano.

The most important intellectual influence, however, which Leone owed to his exile in Italy was that of the Florentine Academy and especially of Pico della Mirandola, at whose personal instigation he wrote the already mentioned book, *De Coeli Harmonia*. It was due to this that Leone became a platonizing Jew in the same way as the members of the Florentine Academy were platonizing Christians, and just as Pico and others had studied the ancient Hebrew literature, so Leone does not show himself averse to Christianity. But though the first and second Aldine editions of the *Dialoghi di Amore* describe the author as "Leone Medico, di Natione Hebreo, et dipoi fatto Christiano" (the third and fourth have merely "Leone Medico Hebreo"), there is no reason to believe that Leone was ever converted to Christianity, and a passage of Christian colouring in the third dialogue may be an interpolation.

Perhaps it was this environment—the best-known Platonic environment—which paradoxically prevented Leone from becoming a thorough Platonist, for in the opinion of the Accademia Platonica, and in Leone's opinion too, there could be but one truth, and so "the philosopher" is both Plato and Aristotle.

With the Renaissance a new truth, that of antiquity, came into being, but the Bible remained the publication of God's word. From this results the emphasis laid by the humanists on harmonizing, on discovering in both the expression of the same divine will. Many of the greatest concordances of that time rest on the magnificent thought that all philosophies, all religions, are manifestations of one divine spirit: Plato and others are no longer pagan authorities for practical wisdom, but the prophets of the same truth of which the greatest prophet was Christ. So men dreamed of a universal religion, grounded in philosophy, in which Christianity, Mohamme-danism and Heathendom should all be absorbed. The desire for that synthesis did not last long, but it still finds an echo in Ficino. It was Ficino's desire to free philosophy from impiety by means of religion, and religion from ignorance by means of philosophy. By way of Platonism he wished to bring back to the faith those whom philosophy had alienated. But by religion he never thought so much of Christianity as of some ideal universal religion, comprehending all creeds, founded on principles common to all men in whom religious principles of any kind exist. Plato was the most likely man to reconcile religion and philosophy, for he had kept an eye on divine things while other philosophers had busied themselves mainly with natural and human concerns. The neo-Platonists of Alexandria had explained his doctrines in the light of Christianity, and Ficino believed with St Augustine that Plotinus, Proclus and Iamblichus appropriated Christian theories as to the divine mind, the nature of the angels and other points. Thus he ended in a platonization of Christianity which was dangerous for Christianity because it made it but one component, even if it were the chief component, of the common natural religion.

That which opened up the way for the general acceptance of Renaissance Platonism in Spain, for example, was Leone Ebreo's combination of the Old Testament with Platonic doctrines, evidence of which is to be found in many passages of the third dialogue. The following is an interesting example of this. After repeating Plato's myth of the Androgynes, Philone tells Sophia that Plato took this fable from Moses's account of the creation of Adam, but the Mosaic description is less detailed and particularized, whereas Plato, when he took it, filled it out and embellished it in accordance with Greek oratory. There is, however, a notable contradiction in the Mosaic story of man's creation: first of all, Moses says that God created Adam on the sixth day, male and female; later, God says "Adam is not well alone, let us make him a mate like him and call that mate woman". This was done by taking one of Adam's ribs as he slept. Thus woman was not made at the beginning, as was said. At the end Moses, relating Adam's progeny, says God made him in the divine similitude, male and female, and called the name of them Adam.

It appears then that they were male and female first and not made so afterwards on account of the subtraction of the rib, for Moses says that when God created Adam, he made him both male and female and called the name of both Adam, making no mention of Eve, which is the name of the female. And afterwards, Adam being alone, God created woman from his side and called her name Eve.

Leone's explanation is that Adam when he was created was androgynous,[1] and that Adam and Eve being in one body, one name, Adam, sufficed. (From this Plato took his myth of the Androgynes who were half male, half female.) Then after that, God said that it was not good that man should be alone, "let us make him a helpmeet like him": that is to say, it was better that woman should be divided from man and face him, instead of looking in the opposite

[1] Cf. *Gen. R.* viii, § 1, ed. Theodor, p. 55.

direction. So God first brought the animals along to see if any of their females would do for Adam, but Adam found none suitable. So God sent him to sleep and took one of his sides (the word for side and rib being equivocal in Hebrew (*sela'*)), that is, divided the female from the male and after the division called the name of the female Eve. Then when Adam awoke, God presented Eve to him, saying that she was flesh of his flesh, and so on.

Thus the only difference between Plato and Moses, as Leone points out, is that Moses says the division was for the better, and that man sinned after the division by eating the apple of the tree of knowledge, whereas Plato says man sinned first through pride and was then divorced from himself. But, Leone contends, Plato did not wish to contradict the Scriptures for we can truthfully affirm that man's division causes him to sin, and that while he is united he has no such inclination. So, since sin and division of man are practically the same thing, or two things inseparable and convertible, we can say that from division came sin, like the Holy Scriptures, and that from sin came division, like Plato.

If a dispute should arise between Plato and Aristotle, Plato's way is almost invariably followed because it also tallies with the theology of Moses. Aristotle, unlike Plato, was not acquainted, says Leone, with the teaching of the ancient Jewish theologians and refused to believe what he could not see for himself, and although he was subtle, his mind in abstract matters was unable to attain the heights reached by Plato's. Leone, following the general belief of the Middle Ages, thought that Plato studied the books of Jewish wisdom when he was in Egypt.

Leone's attempts to harmonize Plato and Moses, though they may sometimes appear far-fetched and do not always tally in detail, are always interesting. Leone was the disciple of the great Florentines, and his attempts at harmonization reveal the tendency of the age, but sometimes he feels called upon to impugn Plato's argument, and then he says that although he is Plato's friend, he is a greater friend to truth. The result of this noble endeavour to ascertain the truth was

bound to be eclecticism in philosophy, for authority was not
to be spurned. Attempting this, the Italians failed to produce
a concord worthy of their own satisfaction, and there resulted
that rupture between a man's intimate life and a man's public
life which has always been noticed by those who have concerned themselves with the Italian Renaissance. But in
Leone there is no such rupture and for him there can be but
one truth. This, says Gebhardt, results from that which is the
common lot of the Jew, a double existence:

> Das Leben in zwei Welten, das das eigentümliche Schicksal des
> Juden ist, führt hier, indem die andere nichtjüdische Welt tiefer
> und in voller Hingegebenheit erlebt wird, zu einer Verschmelzung
> von überzeugender Einheit. Darum gibt es für die Naivität
> Leones, durch die er vielen christlichen Zeitgenossen überlegen
> ist, keine veritas duplex. "Die Wahrheit kann der Wahrheit
> nicht entgegengesetzt sein, und man muss der einen oder der
> anderen Raum geben." Wo Ficino und Pico harmonisieren ist
> bei Leone ursprüngliche Harmonie.

In 1495 Naples was seized by the French and Leone Ebreo
went with his wife to Genoa. Since Genoa at this time could
not compare with many other Italian cities as a cultural
centre, it is probable that he chose it on account of its large
Jewish population, for next to Naples it had received the
greatest number of refugees from Spain. Here, in Genoa, he
began the *Dialoghi di Amore*, which, though not published till
after his death, brought him no little credit in his lifetime
among his own friends.

In 1501 there is news of Leone at Barletta in Apulia. In
the following year he returned to Naples, from which the
French had been driven by Fernández de Córdoba, the Gran
Capitán. In the meantime death had robbed him of his
second son, Samuel, at the age of five, and in Naples, in 1503,
he composed an elegy in Hebrew bewailing his fate, separated
still from his eldest son Isaac.

In 1505 and 1507 there is mention of Leone as the personal
physician of the Viceroy of Naples, Fernández de Córdoba.
In 1505 he visited his father who had settled in Venice, and
there composed the dedicatory verses to three short works of

his father's, published, in the same year, in Constantinople. In 1507 he paid another visit to Venice, and in the next year, that of his father's death, composed an elegy in his memory.

In 1516 he is again mentioned as doctor to the Viceroy of Naples. In the year 1520 he is named, in a privilege of the Emperor Charles V, as being alone exempt from a tribute levied on all the Jews of Naples. In the same year he composed his last work, an introductory poem to his father's commentary on the last prophets, published at Pesaro in 1520. In the following year he was called as an important medical authority to the bedside of Cardinal Sangiorgio: and in the same year there is information that he used his influence with the Viceroy on behalf of the Jews of Naples who were in danger of being banished from there, too, as a result of the preaching of a fanatical Franciscan.

Leone's death probably occurred shortly afterwards, certainly long before 1535, the year in which Mariano Lenzi, a humanist of the circle of the younger Pico della Mirandola, published at Rome the *Dialoghi di Amore* which, he says, had fallen into an almost complete oblivion, from which they should be rescued on account of their own excellence and the renown their author enjoyed during his lifetime.

In 1884 the Spanish literary historian Menéndez y Pelayo produced the theory that Leone Ebreo had written his dialogues originally in Spanish, which Menéndez y Pelayo claimed to be his mother tongue. This view was supported by a statement in the prologue which Carlos Montesa wrote for his Spanish translation of the *Dialoghi*, 1584, in which he says that they were written originally in Spanish; and by certain Hispanicisms in the Italian. But Spanish, in any case, can scarcely be considered Leone's mother tongue, since he was presumably well over twenty before he left Portugal.

Further evidence is supplied in a letter of Tolomei Claudio of the year 1543, in which he admires the excellent style of the *Dialoghi*, adding that this would have been even better if the Italian translation had been equal in clarity to the original.

Modern scholars, Savino and Saitta, have upheld the view that the *Dialoghi* were written in Italian, and for lack of any more definite evidence that view is now generally accepted. The theory most recently put forward—that of the authors of the first English version (1937) of the *Dialoghi di Amore*—is that the work was composed in Ladino—Castilian indited in Hebrew characters. They point out that the British Museum manuscript of the *Dialoghi* written in Ladino, though not contemporary, may well represent Leone's original. A comparison with the first Italian edition has yet to be made.

The *Dialoghi di Amore*, once published, proved extraordinarily popular. Within twenty years of the first Roman edition, five other editions were published in Italy; a Latin translation was published at Venice; there were two French translations and no less than three separate Spanish translations, one of which, by the Inca Garcilaso, has the fame of being the first book published by an American. Most of these translations passed into more than one edition. Finally, a Hebrew translation was made by an Italian Jew, possibly Leo of Modena, in the late sixteenth century.

One of the most ostensible reasons for the popularity of Leone's work in Italy and in Spain was that it was so much more profound and built upon a so much broader basis than the generality of "trattati di amore". But his work was cast in that form, and it therefore made a double appeal, as philosophy and as literature. (This was one of the many assets of dialogue.) Leone had not cared to embed his theories in a learned commentary on an ancient author, from which most people would never take the trouble to extract them, but had cast them in the most popular literary form of the age. Thus to philosophers, Leone seemed the first of their number to free them from the trammels of authority, and to society he came as the first profound thinker to put before it a philosophy which was altogether acceptable and which might serve as a basis for action. So he was accepted, and sometimes even preferred to such as Ficino and Plato himself, on account of his greater intelligibility. On the other hand, it is doubtful whether the triumph of Platonism was due in so large a measure to Leone as Gebhardt would have it:

Nicht in der wissenschaftlich-pedantischen Darstellung Ficinos oder in der eklektischen Compilation Picos, sondern in der poetischen Gestaltung Leones hat der Platonismus die Zeit beherrscht.

Many things contributed to the triumph of Plato, and if in Spain that triumph was very largely due to the *Dialoghi di Amore*, in Italy Leone's was but one work among many, though now it seems one of the most important.

As in the treatises of the day, the chief object of his study is love. The theory of love and the conception of beauty were the chosen themes of Italian society, and it was these themes which Leone's work popularized in Spain. Platonism may have been the fashionable philosophy of the Renaissance and also the form in which many of the greatest Italian artists expressed themselves, but that would never have made Platonism as such popular in Spain, had not Leone given a religious (not necessarily a Christian) turn to these theories of love and beauty. As he himself says in the last *Dialogue*, he takes a wider view of love than Plato did, for Plato spoke only of human love and used his myth to explain the human occurrence. Leone uses myths (this, too, a service to Plato against Aristotle and Aquinas), the myths of the Bible and of the ancients, believing that in them, in allegory, was contained all truth both physical and metaphysical, moral and eschatological. Love, then, for Leone becomes the mainspring of the earth's commotion, that which induces and ordains the harmony of the universe. In Leone's hands, the hard and fast hierarchy of the medieval world is moved and lives through love; or in Pflaum's words: "die mittelalterliche Substanzialität setzt sich in Funktionalität um". Nature then for Leone is the scene of love's action. But we have not yet arrived at the period of Bruno, Campanella and others, and Leone betrays no interest in theories of Nature for their own sake: any ontological conception he may hold is the setting only of his metaphysical system, and with anything approaching pantheism his name cannot justly be connected.

The dialogues occur between a man Philone (love or appetite) and the woman he loves, Sophia (knowledge), but these are scarcely real people. They speak, in the first dialogue, of the nature of love; in the second, of the ubiquity of love; and in the third, of the origin of love, considering, in turn, the questions if, when, where, of whom, why love was born. The methodical aspect of the plan, sufficient to put it at once upon a philosophical basis, and the nature of the questions asked, eminently such as were continually debated in the salons of the sixteenth century, in combination, assured the work of its popularity. But there were many things here to appeal to people outside social cliques accustomed to propose and answer the sort of questions Leone proposes and answers here. There was much here to appeal to the mystic, the graded elevation of carnal love into divine love, the conciliatory attitude, the deeply religious tone of the whole work; there was much to appeal to those interested in the plastic arts, in an age which made of aesthetics an intellectual discipline, in Leone's theory of the nature of beauty in which he definitely abandons the Renaissance conception of beauty as consisting in the proportion of the parts to the whole, and declares that a simple body can be beautiful; much also to appeal to the musical reader in an age when Plato's theories about music were treated with a new respect and vigorously applied; and much to appeal to the philosophical poet (then one impregnated with Platonism), for Leone's work was no narrow or dogmatic statement of opinion, but a philosophy remarkable for a peculiarly elevated idealism fit to impress men still.

For Leone, love is the principle of the universe and, at the same time, the explanation of the cosmic process. Like men, animals are moved by love in their care for their offspring, in their herd instincts. Plants, too, participate in this love. The elements combine through the same elective affinity. The heavenly bodies revolve for love, and love is the principle of gravity.

The created world resulted from the love of Matter for the Forms which inform it, and God, its creator, is the greatest artist. Thus the universe is one individual (and the analogy between the macrocosm and the microcosm is drawn by Leone in the greatest detail). Love is the cosmic principle which is at work in every part of the universe, making it one whole. Thus all things must possess in some measure a soul.

Since love stipulates previous knowledge there must be in all things, in greater or less degree, an intellect. With the principle of love, the basic thought of his Platonism, Leone combines the Aristotelian precept of the "intellectus agens". The understanding is potential only until the "intellectus agens" enlightens it, making actual its knowledge. In this actualization of the understanding is found its true end and the source of its greatest joy. The "intelletto attuale" is one with God, and therefore the highest act of knowledge is knowledge of God. Thus man's desire for knowledge becomes desire for union with God—"deificatio".

God created the world out of love for his own beauty, and the world must return to God who made it. This can occur only through what Leone calls the "amore intellettuale di Dio". Thus, through the return of the soul to God, the universe is eventually joined again to its creator. This, the "fruitio Dei" is the final end of all love, that which the "amorous circle of the universe" strives after in its revolutions.

In the Middle Ages there is a gap between the ecclesiastical conception of love and the worldly conception of love, between "caritas" and "cupiditas", which can scarcely be bridged: sacred love is good, profane love, though necessary, is evil. With the rise of the troubadours in the twelfth century, there comes a change in this outlook on love, but it is a change which brings about no basic alteration. Under Arabic influence, worldly love is sublimated to a chaste affection for worldly things, but human love and divine love are still incompatible and indeed seem to be mutually exclusive. The originality of the Italian school of "dolce stil nuovo", which represented, in many ways, an Italianization of the precepts of the troubadours, lies in the fact that they felt this contrast to be false and attempted to turn human love from the oppositional path to love of God which it had hitherto followed into an imitation of love of God. To top the "dolce stil nuovo" comes Petrarch, but Petrarch brings with him all the wealth of a highly developed individuality and a very great personal sensibility to natural beauty, and his writings represent a notable break with scholasticism. But the amorous casuistry of the "dolce stil nuovo" had been based on philosophical, and, in particular, scholastic, speculation, and if Petrarch was successfully to supersede the writers of that school, it was necessary that he should do it along lines of philosophical reasoning. This he does not do, for his work is based on powers of feeling and intuition. It was not until the works of Plato became more widely known and read that the rift was mended by putting upon an intellectual and philosophical basis that which many people had for long felt to be true.

The *Symposium* seemed to harmonize human with divine love, it had an obvious social application, and for the mystics it provided a scientific process of union. Aristotle's idea of love as desire for possession of an object judged to be good was no longer enough; the new conception of love is intimately bound up with the idea of union with the loved object. The emphasis has ceased to be psychological and has become mystical.

The fullest exposition during the Renaissance of a doctrine of love is to be found in Leone Ebreo's *Dialoghi di Amore*. Here are detailed all the stations of love. The first part of the work is devoted to an analysis of the relationship between love and desire. The author begins by taking over Plato's division of love into three kinds, bestial, human, and divine, and reconciles it with Aristotle's division of love into delectable, useful, and noble. Desire is defined as an affect of the will to be or to have the object which is judged good; love, as an affect of the will to enjoy with union the object which is judged good. The reason for the difference in the three kinds of love and desire is the different nature of the objects which can be loved—delectable, useful, or noble.

Leone Ebreo said that love presupposes knowledge of the object. Love can therefore be defined as desire to enjoy with union that which is known to be good; and although desire presupposes absence of the desired object, yet even if that object exists and is possessed it can still be desired, with a desire not to have it, for it is already possessed, but to enjoy it with comprehending union. Such is the fruition which is desired. This desire is called love, and is of things not possessed which are desired, or of things possessed which it is wished to enjoy with union, or of conversion of the subject by union into the loved object.

The union of bodies is the outward sign of love, and it is natural that, the minds being united in spiritual love, the bodies should wish to partake of that union so that no division should remain. Perfect love between man and woman may now be defined as conversion of the lover into the beloved, with the desire that the beloved may be converted into the lover, and when such love is equal in both parties it is defined as conversion of one lover into the other.

In his third dialogue, however, Leone Ebreo gives a new and wider definition of love. Love in general means desire of something. But love, it has already been said, is not always desire of something, desire being of that which is lacking. The lack, on the other hand, may not be of the actual object, but of perfect union with it, or it may be that the lover possesses and enjoys the object at the moment, but lacks such enjoyment in the future, and for that reason desires it. In general, then, desire and love are the same, although it is customary to draw some distinction between them. Enjoyment, then, is of what is possessed; love is of what is lacking and is one with desire. But that which is possessed is loved and obviously is not lacking. In this case it is true that the present possession is there, but continual possession in the future is lacking, and this is loved and desired by him who is enjoying present happiness. Present possession is what is enjoyed; future possession is what is desired and loved. This is what led Plato to define love as the desire to possess that which is deemed good, and to possess it always, for in the "always" is included continual lack of it.

This, however, would not appear to be applicable to the

love of God for created things, any lack being incompatible with the concept of the Divinity. But as in human relationships not only the inferior loves the superior, but the superior loves the inferior, hoping to perfect him, so is the case also in divine love and desire. Man loves God and desires God; God not only loves man but desires him too. But God lacks nothing: why should God love and desire that which is faulty? This was Plato's difficulty too, and it was this which made him contend that the gods were without love and that love was not a god, because love being, as he defines it, desire for a beautiful object which is lacking, it is impossible that the gods, who are most beautiful and without fault, should have it.

But Plato in his *Symposium* deals only with that sort of love which in men terminates in the lover, but not in the beloved, though the latter has most right to the title of love, and the other is more fitly called friendship. This Plato rightly defines as desire for beauty, and says that such love is not found in God, because he who desires beauty neither possesses it nor is beautiful, and God, who is consummately beautiful, cannot lack beauty nor desire it. That kind of love, therefore, cannot be found in God. Leone, however, who speaks of love in general, necessarily treats both of the love which terminates in the lover and presupposes lack in the lover, and of the love which terminates in the beloved and presupposes lack in the beloved and not in the lover. It is for this reason that he did not define love as desire for a beautiful thing, but only as desire for something. Plato says further, speaking of this second kind of love, that good and wise men are the friends of God, and God loves them, desiring their perfection. The name of love may therefore be applied to any desire, though, in particular, it is applied only to desire for a beautiful object. Thus Plato did not exclude all love from God, but only that which is desire for beauty. The love of God for man is therefore the desire of the Creator to perfect his creature.

At this point the necessity of knowledge is to be enjoined, for it is not only lack of beauty in man, but consciousness of that lack which engenders love and desire for beauty. (This is the meaning of Plato's fable of Plenty and Poverty.) Thus the father of all love in the lower world is knowledge of beauty, and the mother is lack of beauty, and the common father of all love is the beautiful, and the common mother is knowledge of that beauty together with lack of it. These are the parents of love and desire, because the beautiful, when known by him who lacks beauty, is at once loved and desired, and love is thus engendered by the beautiful in the understanding of him who knows it and who lacks it and desires it. Thus the beloved plays the part of the father, and the lover of the mother who conceives and desires what Plato calls generation in beauty. The lover is therefore not entirely without the beauty of the beloved, for he does at least know it, and even if union is not perfected, he still is not deprived of intellectual cognizance of the form and exemplar of the beauty he desires and which he lacks. There are, moreover, two kinds of knowledge: one is imperfect, is presupposed by love, and has love as its ultimate end; the other is perfect, succeeds love, and is the ultimate end of love. But it must not be forgotten that, in the intellectual nature, understanding and love are one and can be distinguished only rationally. Unitive fruition is the most perfect stage of both. Love and desire are therefore the means of guiding us from imperfect knowledge to perfect unitive understanding.

Though the first and imperfect kind of knowledge is presupposed by love, it cannot alone engender love. Love is an affect of the will, and before love can come into being, the understanding must depute its powers to the will. The understanding when it understands makes things like itself, so that material things become intellectual; the will, on the contrary, when it loves things makes itself like them. The will thus takes the form of the beloved object. The will is, moreover, the most potent of the three "potentiae" of the soul, and if love draws the will after it, the will draws after it the whole man, just as the first heaven carries the others round with it in its motion. Since the will has this mastery over man, and love over will, then, where love leads, all must follow, and so the whole man comes to be what he loves, his will being identified with that of the beloved object. The will of the subject is therefore alienated from him and he is no longer governed by it. Similarly, the whole soul of the lover flees from his body and takes up its abode in the body of the beloved.

The flight of the will after the loved object, and of all other human faculties after the will, which is their overlord, is the cause of the extraordinary effects of love which may be seen in the lover. Love is certainly born of reason, but it is not limited nor guided by it. Unreason and disorderliness are as much a characteristic of noble as of ignoble love, and what love is more noble than the love of God, and what love is more boundless and ardent?

But the most remarkable effect of love is the transformation of the lover into the beloved. This metamorphosis occurs by virtue of the power of love and is not the result of violence nor of force, but is voluntary and delightful, and the fusion of the two into one is so perfect and so just that no force can part them, provided they remain unchanged in affection and in will. This transformation represents the consummation of love.

From human love man rises to divine love. Since the lover is transformed into that which he loves, if that which he loves is strong, he will be strong; if noble, he will be noble; if virtuous, he will be virtuous. Therefore the better the love-object, the better the man will be who loves it. And because God is infinitely powerful, infinitely good, infinitely beautiful, if man makes God the chief object of his love he will partake in his soul of the attributes of the Deity.

Since man becomes like the object of his love, it is of evident importance that he should love only that which is superior to him, and understand that which is inferior to him, that he himself may become like that which he loves, and may make like himself that which he understands. Granted that the understanding makes its objects like itself, and the will becomes like its objects, this is the way to attain intellectual and spiritual perfection.

Leone Ebreo, however, makes a most notable addition to this conception. He says that by loving not only that which is superior to him, but also that which is inferior, man increases in perfection and approaches more nearly to the perfection of God, for the superior not only increases in perfection by doing good to the inferior, but also adds to the perfection of the universe, which is the final end of all love. Through this increase of perfection in the lover and in the universe, the inferior beloved partakes of divinity in the superior lover, because in so far as the inferior, though inferior, is loved, he participates in the divinity of the Creator who is the primal and consummate Beloved, by participation in whom all that is loved is divine. All that is beautiful participates in the consummate Beauty of God, and the lover who loves that which is beautiful, even though it is inferior to him, approaches more nearly to God. The lover increases thereby in beauty and divinity, and this increase goes to swell the increase of the universe, too, in those same qualities of beauty and divinity. That which at first sight is marked as inferior owing to lack and privation of beauty, being further removed from the consummate beauty of the Creator, is thus made by Leone to contribute to and to increase the sum of that universal love which is the motor of the world. Nothing exists to which love is extraneous: in men and animals love is a passion; in the elements and in lifeless bodies it is a natural inclination. Love is the desire felt by all created things to attain their fit position, in order that the amorous circle of the universe may revolve harmoniously.

This conception of love, which presupposes defect in the lover, for all things lack the divine perfection, is obviously not applicable to the love of God for his creatures. What then is the nature of God's love? God's love is the will to do good to his creatures and the universe and to perfect them as far as their given nature will allow. Such love presupposes fault not in the lover but in the beloved. God rejoices in the good which he does his creatures, but such joy is not absolute, but relative only to the creatures, just as the defect (which gives rise to desire) is not absolute in God, but relative only to the creatures. This relative perfection in God is the end of the love which God bears the universe. It is on this account that

God produces and maintains all things. Thus the man who loves that which is inferior to him, hoping to perfect it, plays a divine part, parallel to that which God plays in the universe.

There are therefore two alternatives, both admirable, open to the man who loves. If he loves that which is inferior to him, he plays a parallel part to that of the Divinity; if he loves that which is superior to him, he may rise from love of human things to love of divine things, finally being transformed into God. With Leone, love has become a theological and a cosmological system. Love is the means of spiritual betterment; it is the means of universal preferment.

The *Dialoghi di Amore* as they stand are incomplete. The last words of the third dialogue show unmistakably that Leone intended to add a fourth—and probably final—discourse, which should treat of the effects of love. No doubt this was never written. An undertaking to write such a fourth dialogue of the effects of love was later made by Alessandro Piccolomini in the prologue to his *Institutione di tutta la vita dell' uomo nato nobile*. But this, too, it appears, was never actually written.

In Italy almost every subsequent writer of a "trattato di amore" came under the influence of Leone Ebreo. Varchi mentions him with admiration and respect; Betussi refers to the learned Jew; Tullia d'Aragona, in her *Della Infinità di Amore*, says she prefers him to Plato and Ficino on account of his greater intelligibility; Tasso, in his *Minturno*, where he speaks against the Renaissance definition of beauty as the proportion of the parts to the whole, may well have been influenced by Leone. But the profound and truly poetic qualities of the *Dialoghi di Amore* escaped these Italian admirers. Their treatises are taken up with the casuistry of love; with discussion of "questions" as in Betussi's *Raverta*; at best, with paeans to love and ideal beauty, the model for which was provided by the *Cortegiano*. It is their mood which is Platonic, rather than their essential content. They mention Leone Ebreo's name; they borrow an idea or two without letting their mind revolve upon it, without making it their own; they even copy out passages, almost word for word.

Consequently it is not difficult to trace the influence of Leone Ebreo in Italy, for his ideas and their expression, even after digestion by another, undergo very little change.

It was in Spain that the *Dialoghi di Amore* bore most fruit, and Christoval Acosta, a sixteenth-century writer, expressly mentions them as one of the two chief sources for the theory of Platonic love in that country. Here, too, wholesale plagiarisms were effected, though in Spain they were not acknowledged as they usually had been in Italy. Montemayor in his pastoral novel *Diana* copied many passages word for word from the first of the *Dialoghi di Amore*; Maximiliano Calvi's *Tratado de la hermosura y del amor* is virtually a transcription of Leone Ebreo but completely reshuffled, so that the first dialogue is on beauty, the second on love, and the third an attack on Cupid; Cervantes, in his pastoral *La Galatea*, took much verbatim from the same source.

But it was on the mystics and religious poets and prose-writers of Spain, on such men as Luis de León and Malón de Chaide, that the influence of Leone Ebreo fell with happiest result. Ficino himself had leanings towards mysticism, and indeed Renaissance Platonism is mystical, in the Plotinian tradition, rather than intellectual, in the Platonic tradition, though "the philosopher" is always Plato. If that is so in Italy, it is so, to an even greater extent, in Spain. Ficino was descended from the school of Alexandria only, as it were, on one side; Leone Ebreo on two, for he represents a collaboration of the Spanish Semitic philosophy of ibn Gabirol and Maimonides with the Platonic Academy of Florence, the common source of both being Plotinus and the Alexandrian school. Leone speaks always of Plato, but it is a habit he picked up in Italy. The apex of his philosophical system, as the apex of that of Plotinus, is the union of the soul with God. The means by which that union is effected is perfect love, but love cannot be perfect unless it is based on perfect knowledge. The most perfect knowledge, in kind as well as in degree, is knowledge of God; God being the *summum bonum* is also necessarily the final end of love: thus, from both aspects, union with God is the final end of all being.

This is the doctrine of Leone Ebreo, and it is easy to understand the attraction it had for the Christian mystics of Spain, for it seemed to provide mysticism with a philosophy. Leone was something of a mystic himself and certainly favourable to that condition which makes union with the Divinity a possibility in this life. There are many passages in his work which mark him as the forerunner of the Spanish mystics of the last half of the century. There is a passage in the first dialogue, in which he speaks most expressly of the process of mystical union. Here are set out all the grades requisite in Spanish mysticism: the starting-point of knowledge, which sets the whole upon an intellectual basis; the love induced by that knowledge, which leads the soul to desire union with the Divinity; the reciprocated love of God for the soul, revealed in the gift of grace; the renewed effort and the consummating union. But still there is desire, for love breeds desire, not for a more perfect union, which is impossible, but for a repetition of that life-giving moment. Such moments represent the supreme felicity of man; such deification is his final end.

In the third dialogue come other passages enlarging upon the details of the mystic's trance: the effect upon the physical condition of the patient of this spiritual ecstasy; his complete transformation. This is a recurrence of Plato's theory of the transformation of the lover into the beloved and it provided Spanish mysticism (and mystics of other countries) with an admirable account of the process of union of the human soul with God. Sometimes desire for union may be so pungent and contemplation so ecstatic that the soul frees itself entirely from the body and becomes one with the desired and contemplated object, leaving the body behind lifeless and inanimate. This is how Moses and Aaron died.

But knowledge, and here Leone is most emphatic, is the necessary preliminary to any love productive of union, and since man cannot obtain perfect knowledge of God, God of his grace enables the aspiring man to realize something of the nature of the Divinity. (This he explains by a simile from human love, for the man would never attain to that delectable union, which is the aim of his affection, if the woman with sweet words and amorous glances did not first prove herself complacent.) To Christian readers, this must have seemed a remarkable affirmation in a philosophic work of the Christian doctrine of grace, and since it came from one who was not himself among the faithful, a refutation, doubly valid, of disbelief. The mystics, some of whom were temperamentally inclined to try to eliminate the first steps in the Platonic ladder from physical to spiritual, and to attain at once to a knowledge of things unseen, found a convenient means in the doctrine of grace, and here again they were aided by Leone Ebreo. Leone says that the reason, the rational soul, can know spiritual beauty only by way of physical beauty, but the pure intellect, that is the intellect of the mystic no longer hindered by the flesh, can know intuitively the beauty of the Divinity, which is for man beatitude.

The reduction of man to his Creator is but a parallel on a small scale of the reduction of the universe to God from whom it emanated. Thus the end of the universal love being union with the Creator, he who plays the greatest part in attaining this end is the mystic.

It is of interest to note the possible influence of Leone Ebreo on such a writer as Juan de los Angeles who, it seems, was not himself an empirical mystic. Rather than one of the actual conquerors of the spiritual Kingdom of God, Juan de los Angeles was the organiser of victory. In the second part of his *Lucha Espiritual y Amorosa entre Dios y el Alma* there is a specific description of the amorous struggle between God and the soul. There is all the paraphernalia of the "mirada", the arrows of love and the chains, and many other things which are to be found in the poets and lay writers of the period, but besides this, the sickness, the insatiability, the swoon, the mortification, the union and the transformation of lover into beloved, which lift it on to a higher plane, the love of the soul for God. Such a combination of sacred and profane love, the second exemplifying the first, the first enlightening the second (as in Titian's painting) seems typical of Leone Ebreo, and not precisely the course that would be taken by an apologian of mysticism on his own account.

Elsewhere he speaks of the many notable things Diotima said of love in Plato's *Symposium*, one of them being that it caused illness. This, says Juan de los Angeles, is because all the virtue of the natural complexion follows the mind to the beloved object. The stomach fails to absorb the food owing to the resultant lack of heat, and most of it is excreted. There follows a shortage of blood which causes weakness and infirmity. This is very comparable to Leone Ebreo's description of the physical effects of the mystic's trance, but it would be unwise to seek a direct influence on a point like this which represented the common medical philosophy of the day.

There are, however, passages in the works of Juan de los Angeles which reflect a less dubious influence of Leone's work. In a passage in the *Triunfos del Amor de Dios* he uses words which seem to reflect Leone's conception of the amorous circle of the universe. His idea is perhaps Plotinian in origin, but his emphasis on the circle (the circle, the mobile figure, and not the sphere, is considered most perfect), though the weight of that emphasis is changed, seems to be an echo of what he may well have read in the *Dialoghi di Amore*. After Philone has exposed this conception in the *Dialoghi* Sophia says that she now understands the admirable circle of being, and although he has already explained it to her before, it so satisfies and delights her mind that it seems ever novel. And eternally interesting it must have seemed to others besides Sophia, for so poetic an idea had scarcely been conceived since the time of Dante.

Even more certainly under a debt to Leone is a passage from the *Lucha* which expresses the idea that the lover equivalates to the woman in human love (to the soul in divine love) and the beloved to the man (in divine love to God) which is not one which would occur to all, and which indeed on the face of it is paradoxical. But Leone, in whom this idea appears to originate, has a very sufficient explanation for it, and there can be little doubt that Juan de los Angeles took it from the *Dialoghi*, though it has become altered in the process.

In France, the *Dialoghi di Amore* influenced both the poetic school of Lyons, the leader of which, Pontus de Tyard, was one of the translators of the *Dialoghi* into French, and the Pléiade, chiefly through Maurice Scève, whose chief work *Délie*, being an anagram of the word *l'idée*, is typical of the idealistic elements introduced, largely as a result of Leone Ebreo's influence on Scève, into French poetry at this time. But the French proved sceptical, and the influence of Leone here was not of long duration: Montaigne, in one of his essays, has some caustic remarks to make about the theory of love exemplified in the *Dialoghi di Amore*; and Ronsard, in one of his sonnets, is positively rude to Leone. Despite this reaction, however, which is to be seen also in Italy in the work of many burlesque poets, and in Spain, in the figure of Cervantes's Dulcinea who ate garlic, the influence of Leone continues into the seventeenth century, chiefly in the pastoral novel (such as d'Urfé's *Astrée*), not one of which could be considered complete without a long disquisition on ideal love and beauty.

In philosophy, Leone's theory of love may have provided the starting-point for the Italian philosophers of the Counter-Reformation, Campanella and Giordano Bruno. Certainly it influenced Spinoza, whose library contained a copy of Leone's work in Spanish: from it he took over the idea and terminology of his *fruitio unitiva* and his *amor dei intellectualis*, though these terms take on a different meaning in Spinoza. The idea of *deificatio*, for instance, with Leone is mystical; with Spinoza, this mystical conception becomes rationalistic.

After this, though Schiller in one of his letters to Goethe says he had come across the Latin Translation of the *Dialoghi* which he read with interest, finding the work of great help in his astrological studies, nobody took any more notice of the *Dialoghi di Amore* until quite recent years when they were rediscovered, but less for their own sake than as an important "source" for Spinoza's philosophy.

BIBLIOGRAPHY

FRANZ DELITZSCH. "Leo der Hebräer," *Literaturblatt des Orients*, Leipzig, 1840.

CARMOLY. *Médecins juifs.*

— *Ozar Nechmad*, II.

GEIGER. *Ibid.*

S. MUNK. *Mélanges de Philosophie juive et arabe*, Paris, 1859. Appendice No. IV. Notice sur Léon Hébreu.

KAYSERLING. *Geschichte der Juden in Portugal*, Berlin, 1867.

Cat. Bodl. 1602.

GRAETZ. *Geschichte der Juden*, IX[4].

MENÉNDEZ Y PELAYO. *Historia de las ideas estéticas en España*, Madrid, 1884.

B. ZIMMELS. *Leo Hebraeus*, Breslau, 1886.

— "Leone Ebreo," *Neue Studien*, I, Wien, 1892.

E. SOLMI. *Benedetto Spinoza e Leone Ebreo*, Modena, 1903.

MENÉNDEZ Y PELAYO. *Orígenes de la novela*, I, Madrid, 1905.

E. APPEL. "Leone Medigos Lehre vom Weltall," *Archiv für Geschichte der Philosophie*, XX, Berlin, 1907.

E. SOLMI, "La data della morte di Leone Ebreo," *Giornale storico della letteratura italiana*, LIII, 1909.

L. SAVINO. *Trattati e trattatisti d'amore del cinquecento*, Napoli, 1914.

B. CROCE. "Un documento su Leone Ebreo," *Critica*, XII, Napoli, 1914.

N. FERORELLI. *Gli Ebrei nell' Italia Meridionale*, Torino, 1915.

J. DE CARVALHO. *Leão Hebreu*, Coimbra, 1918.

C. GEBHARDT. "Spinoza und der Platonismus," *Chronicon Spinozanum*, I, Haag, 1921.

G. SAITTA. "La filosofia di Leone Ebreo," *Giornale critico della filosofia italiana*, Messina-Roma, Anno V, Fascicolo I, 1924; Anno VI, Fascicolo II, 1925; Anno VI, Fascicolo III, 1925.

H. PFLAUM. "Der Renaissance-Philosoph Leone Ebreo," *Soncino-Blätter*, I, Berlin, 1925–6.

— *Die Idee der Liebe. Leone Ebreo. Zwei Abhandlungen zur Geschichte der Philosophie*, Tübingen, 1926.

G. SAITTA. *Filosofia italiana e Umanesimo* (cap. "La filosofia di Leone Ebreo"), Venezia, 1928.

Leone Ebreo: *Dialoghi d' amore, Hebräische Gedichte*, herausgegeben von Carl Gebhardt, Heidelberg, 1929. (*Bibliotheca Spinozana*, III.)